A TEXT BOOK OF SOFTWARE ENGINEERING

Harish Kumar Mittal

Principal, B. M. Institute of Engineering & Technology, Sonepat

Third Edition, 2025

Printed in India

Made on the Notion Press Platform

www.notionpress.com

iii

Dedicated to My Family and Students

TABLE OF CONTENTS

3   COST ESTIMATION AND PROJECT PLANNING . 91

1 INTRODUCTION

The evolution of modern computing began in the 1940s with the first electronic digital computers. In the 1970s, the C programming language emerged and quickly became a foundational language for system software, operating systems (such as UNIX), and later many applications that supported the rise of personal computing. The appearance of early microcomputers marked an important milestone, bringing computing power closer to individuals and small organizations.

The term **"software engineering"** was formally introduced in 1968 at a NATO conference in Germany. This reflected the need to treat software development as an engineering discipline, with an emphasis on **quality, cost-effectiveness, maintainability, and systematic processes**.

During the 1970s and 1980s, structured methods and the concept of a **Software Development Life Cycle (SDLC)** became widely adopted. SDLC provided an organized framework for planning, building, testing, and maintaining software systems.

The mid-1990s brought another major turning point with the growth of the **Internet and the www**, which dramatically expanded the scale, connectivity, and impact of software systems. Since then, software engineering has continued to evolve and now underpins almost every aspect of modern life and technology.

1.1 PROGRAM VERSUS SOFTWARE

Before studying software engineering in depth, it is important to distinguish between a **program** and **software**.

Program

A **program** is a set of instructions written in a programming language that a computer can execute. It typically:

- Has a clear starting point (e.g., main() function in C/C++ or Java).

- Takes input, performs computations or operations, and produces some output.

- Focuses mainly on the **executable logic**.

For example, a short C program that reads two numbers and prints their sum is a **program**. Even if it is only a few lines long, it is still a valid program.

Software

Software is a broader term. It usually refers to:

A program or a collection of programs **along with** associated components such as libraries, configuration files, documentation, and sometimes related data, designed together to perform a specific task or provide a service.

Typical components of software include:

- One or more **executable programs**

- **Libraries** or modules used by those programs

- **Configuration files**

- **User documentation** (user manuals, help files, online help)

- **Developer documentation** (design documents, code comments, API docs)

For example, a calculator application with:

- The main calculation logic (program)

- A graphical user interface (buttons, display)

- Help files or user instructions

together form a **software product**.

Key idea: Every program is software, but when we say *software* in software engineering, we usually mean the **complete product**, not just the raw code. **Figure 1** illustrates the typical components that together constitute software.

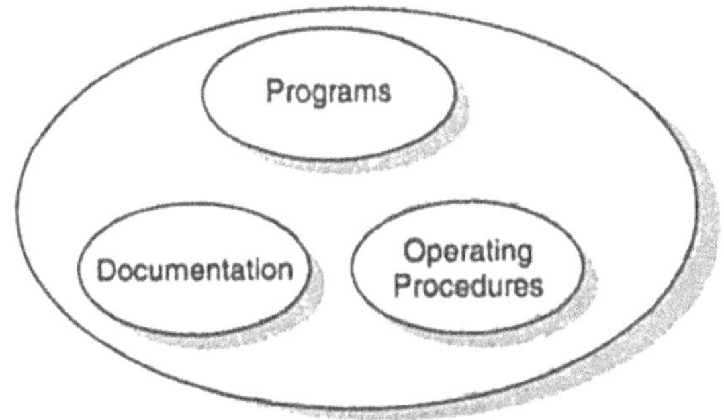

Figure 1: Components of Software (Aggarwal, 2005)

Why is Software Important?

Software is now a critical asset for individuals, organizations, and nations:

- The economies of all developed (and many developing) nations are increasingly **dependent on software** for banking, communication, transport, education, governance, and more.

- A growing number of systems in **military, industrial, medical, educational, and entertainment** domains are **software-controlled**.

- Expenditure on software development, maintenance, and related services forms a **significant portion of the Gross National Product (GNP)** in many countries.

Because of this, the way we **design, build, test, deploy, and maintain software** has a direct impact on reliability, safety, security, and cost at national and global levels.

1.2 ATTRIBUTES OF A GOOD SOFTWARE

A good software product is not judged only by whether it "works". It must also be:

- Functionally correct

- Efficient in its use of resources

- Easy to maintain and evolve

- Safe and secure to use

- Acceptable and usable for its intended users

These are often called **software quality attributes** or **non-functional requirements**.

Essential Attributes of Good Software

- **Maintainability**
  Software should be designed so that it can be **easily modified and extended**. As user needs, business rules, or technology change, developers should be able to fix defects, add new features, and adapt the system without excessive cost or risk.

- **Efficiency**
  Software should use system resources **judiciously—** including processor time, memory, disk space, and network

bandwidth. Efficient software performs its tasks without unnecessary delays or overhead, especially for large-scale or real-time systems.

- **Acceptability (Usability and Compatibility)**
  The software should be:

  - o **Understandable**: users can learn how to use it without excessive training.

  - o **Easy to use**: interface and workflows are user-friendly.

  - o **Compatible**: it works correctly with other systems, platforms, and tools that users rely on.

- **Correctness**
  Software must perform its **intended functions accurately**, according to the specification. Correctness means that for valid inputs, the software produces the expected outputs and behaves as defined in the requirements.

- **Portability**
  Portable software can be **moved from one environment to another** (e.g., from Windows to Linux, or from on-premise servers to the cloud) with minimal changes. This is usually achieved by avoiding platform-specific features or isolating them in well-defined modules.

- **Cost-effectiveness (Budget)**

  Software should be developed and maintained in a **cost-effective** manner. This means balancing:

  - o Required quality and functionality

  - o Time-to-market or delivery deadlines

  - o Available budget and human resources

- **Security**
  Software must protect **data and services against unauthorized access or misuse**. Only authorized users should be able to access the system and its data. Security also includes resistance to attacks, protection of privacy, and safe handling of errors.

In practice, software engineering is largely about **managing trade-offs** between these attributes, based on the priorities of users and stakeholders.

1.3 SOFTWARE MYTHS

In the early days of software development (and even today), many misconceptions—called **software myths**—have affected how managers, customers, and developers think about software projects. These myths often lead to unrealistic expectations and poor decisions. Below are some common myths and their realities:

- **Myth 1: "Software is easy to change." Reality:**
  Changing software is rarely "easy." A small change in one module can:

  - Introduce new bugs.
  - Break existing functionality.
  - Affect performance or security. Proper impact analysis, regression testing, and documentation updates are needed for even seemingly minor changes.

- **Myth 2: "Once software is implemented, the work is done."**

  Reality:
  Software development does **not** end with the first release. In practice, most of the effort over the lifetime of a system goes into:

  - Fixing defects discovered after deployment.

- o Adapting the software to new hardware, platforms, or regulations.
- o Adding new features and improving performance. This is known as **software maintenance and evolution**.

- **Myth 3: "Quality cannot be assessed before testing."**

  Reality:
  Software quality can and should be assessed **throughout** the development process, not only during final testing. Examples include:

  - o **Code reviews and walkthroughs**
  - o **Static analysis tools** (for style, security, and complexity)
  - o **Adherence to coding standards and design principles**
  - o **Early prototyping and design reviews** Testing is essential, but it is only one of many quality assurance activities.

1.4 SOFTWARE EVOLUTION

Software evolution is the continuous process of modifying and updating software after its initial release to:

- Respond to changing user requirements and business rules.

- Fix bugs and security vulnerabilities.

- Improve performance, usability, and reliability.

In **medium to large software projects**, the budget spent on **evolving existing software** is often **greater** than the cost of developing the first version. Reasons include:

- The need to fully understand and safely modify an existing, often complex system.

- Dependencies on other systems, libraries, and legacy technologies.

- The requirement to maintain backward compatibility and avoid breaking current users.

Therefore, software engineering places strong emphasis on **designing software for change**, not just for initial delivery.

1.5 SOFTWARE ENGINEERING

Software Engineering applies **engineering principles and practices** to the development, operation, and maintenance of software systems. The goal is to produce software that is:

- Reliable

- Efficient

- Maintainable

- Delivered on time and within budget

In simple terms:

Software engineering is the **application of engineering to software development**.

A widely used definition from IEEE states:

"Software engineering is the application of a systematic, disciplined, quantifiable approach to the development, operation, and maintenance of software."

Modern software engineering focuses on:

- **High-quality software products** that meet specified functional and non-functional requirements.

- **Process discipline**: using defined methods, models, and tools rather than ad hoc coding.

- **Manageability**: planning, tracking, and controlling cost, schedule, and risks.

It is often observed that **software development can cost more than the hardware** on which it runs. Without proper software engineering practices, large, complex systems are:

- Hard to understand and modify.

- More likely to fail or become unmaintainable.

- Much more expensive over their lifetime.

This is why software engineering is now treated as a full-fledged engineering discipline, similar in seriousness to civil, electrical, or mechanical engineering.

1.6 SOFTWARE CRISIS!

The term **"software crisis"** was used in the 1960s and 1970s to describe the serious difficulties that organizations faced in building large, reliable, and efficient software systems. As the size and complexity of software increased, many projects:

- Failed to meet their requirements.

- Were delivered late or not delivered at all.

- Suffered from poor performance, instability, and large numbers of defects.

Key reasons for the software crisis included:

- Lack of **systematic development methodologies** and formal processes.

- Difficulty in **testing and verifying** large-scale systems.

- Limited access to powerful, affordable computing resources and tools.

These challenges highlighted the need for **better methods, tools, and professional practices**, which led directly to the emergence of software engineering as a distinct discipline.

Key Factors Behind the Software Crisis

- **Larger Problem Sizes**

  Software began to solve much bigger and more complex problems (e.g., real-time control, banking, air-traffic systems), which could not be managed using informal, small-program practices.

- **Lack of Adequate Training**

  The software industry grew faster than the availability of trained professionals. Many programmers had little formal training in structured development or design methods.

- **Increasing Skill Shortage**

  Demand for skilled software engineers far exceeded supply, leading to overworked teams and compromised quality.

- **Low Productivity Improvement**

  Traditional methods and tools did not scale well to large systems, resulting in slow progress and inefficient use of resources.

Problems Associated with the Software Crisis

Typical issues faced in projects during that era (and still seen today in some form) included:

- Failure to fully meet user requirements

- Frequent crashes and unreliability

- Late delivery of software projects

- Non-optimal use of hardware and human resources

- High costs and frequent budget overruns

According to one often-cited IBM report:

- About **31% of projects** were canceled before completion.

- About **53% of projects** exceeded their cost estimates.

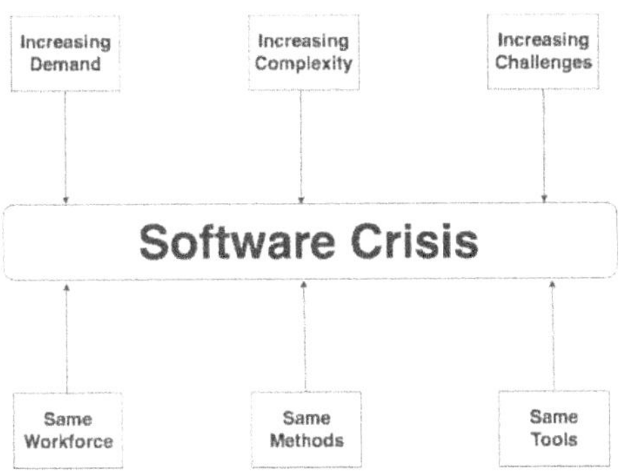

Figure 2: Software Crisis

These statistics clearly demonstrated that traditional, informal approaches to software development were inadequate.

"No Silver Bullet"

Between the 1970s and 1990s, many new technologies and practices—such as high-level languages, structured programming, object-oriented programming, and various tools—were promoted as potential solutions to the software crisis.

However, **Fred Brooks**, in his famous article **"No Silver Bullet"**, argued that:

- No single technology or practice could bring a **tenfold increase in productivity** within a decade.

- There is **no magical solution** ("no silver bullet") that can instantly solve all software development problems.

- Improvements in software development are mostly **incremental**, coming from better processes, tools, experience, and discipline.

This perspective remains highly relevant: software engineering must focus on continuous improvement rather than searching for a miracle cure.

The Year 2000 (Y2K) Problem

The **Y2K problem**, or **"millennium bug,"** is a classic example of how small design decisions can cause global software risks.

- Many older systems stored years using only **two digits** (e.g., 79 for 1979) to save memory.

- When the year changed from 1999 (99) to 2000 (00), some systems could interpret 00 as **1900** instead of 2000.

- This could affect:

    - Date comparisons
    - Interest calculations
    - Scheduling and billing
    - Other time-dependent operations

During the 1990s, it became clear that this issue could cause serious failures in financial, and technical systems worldwide. Governments and organizations spent **huge amounts** to:

- Identify Y2K-sensitive code.
- Correct data formats and logic.
- Test and verify the behavior of critical systems.

The Y2K effort had significant **economic, political, and administrative** implications and is often cited as a large-scale, worldwide software maintenance and risk-management exercise

1.7 SOFTWARE PROCESS

A **software process** is the structured way in which software is developed and evolved. It defines **how** we go from an initial idea or need to a working software product, and how we continue to modify that product over time.

In simple terms, a software process is the **set of activities, methods, and practices** followed during software development. Most software processes include the following core activities:

1. Software Requirements Specification (SRS)

This activity focuses on **what** the software must do. It involves:

- Identifying and documenting required functionalities.

- Capturing constraints (performance, security, legal, hardware limits, etc.).

- Producing a clear, unambiguous **Software Requirements Specification (SRS)**.

A good SRS is essential. If requirements are unclear or incorrect, later stages will suffer, leading to rework, delays, and cost overruns.

2. Design and Coding

Once the requirements are understood, the next step is to decide **how** the software will meet them. This phase usually has two levels:

- **High-level (architectural) design**

  - Defines the overall structure of the system.

  - Identifies major modules, components, and their interactions.

- **Detailed design and coding**

- o Specifies algorithms, data structures, interfaces, and internal logic.

- o Implementation of the design in a programming language (coding).

The outcome is the **source code** of the system, organized according to the chosen design.

3. Verification and Validation (V&V)

Verification and validation ensure that the software is both **correct** and **useful**:

- **Verification** – "Are we building the product right?"

  - o Checks whether the software correctly implements the specified design and requirements.

  - o Activities include reviews, inspections, and various types of testing.

- **Validation** – "Are we building the right product?"

  - o Checks whether the software actually meets the **real needs** of the users and stakeholders.

  - o Involves user acceptance testing, beta trials, and feedback.

Together, V&V ensure that the software **conforms to its specification** and **satisfies user expectations**.

4. Software Maintenance (and Evolution)

After the software is deployed, work does not stop. The system is used in the real world and must be:

- **Corrected** – Fixing defects that surface during operation.

- **Adapted** – Modifying the software for new environments, platforms, or regulations.

- **Enhanced** – Adding new features or improving performance and usability.

This ongoing process is called **software maintenance** and, more broadly, **software evolution**. It often consumes a large portion of the total project budget.

1.8 SOFTWARE LIFE CYCLE (PROCESS) MODELS

A **software process model** (or **software life cycle model**) is a **simplified representation** of the software development process. It shows:

- The main **phases** of development.

- The **order** in which these activities are carried out.

- The typical **deliverables** and checkpoints at each stage.

The main goal of using a process model is to provide a **framework for planning, organizing, and controlling** software projects so that the final product meets its objectives in terms of quality, cost, and schedule.

The choice of a life cycle model can significantly affect:

- Development **costs and risks**.

- Ability to handle **requirement changes**.

- Ease of coordination among team members.

Different models are suitable for different types of projects—small vs large, stable vs evolving requirements, high-risk vs low-risk, etc. The development team must select the model (or combination of models) that best matches the project's context.

In this section, we will briefly discuss several popular software process models, including:

- Build-and-Fix Model

- Waterfall Model

- Prototyping Approach

- Spiral Model

- Iterative Development Process

- Object-Oriented development approaches

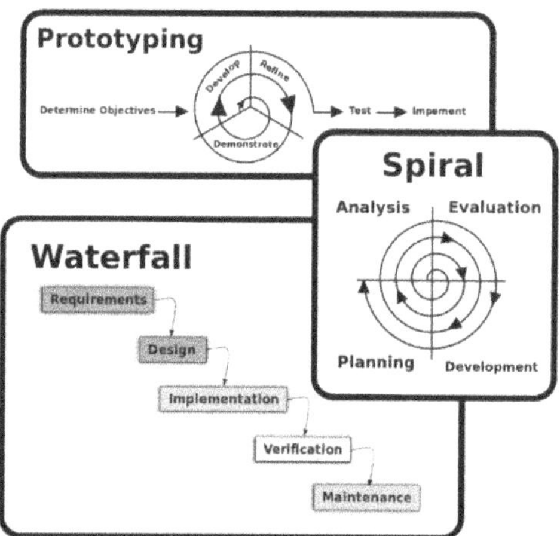

Figure 3: Software Life Cycle (Process) Models

1.8.1   BUILD AND FIX MODEL

The **Build-and-Fix Model** is the most basic and informal way of developing software. The process is essentially:

1. Write some code.

2. Run it and see what happens.

3. Fix problems.

4. Repeat.

There is **no formal specification, design, or documentation**. Changes are made directly in the code whenever issues are found or new requirements appear.

This approach may be acceptable only for:

- Very small programs (e.g., quick utility scripts).

- One-time, throwaway code with little or no need for maintenance.

However, for anything beyond **tiny projects (around 100–200 lines of code)**, the build-and-fix model becomes:

- Hard to maintain and extend.

- Prone to many defects.

- Difficult to estimate in terms of time and cost.

Key limitation: The absence of systematic planning, design, and documentation makes the Build-and-Fix Model **impractical and risky** for real-world, long-lived software systems

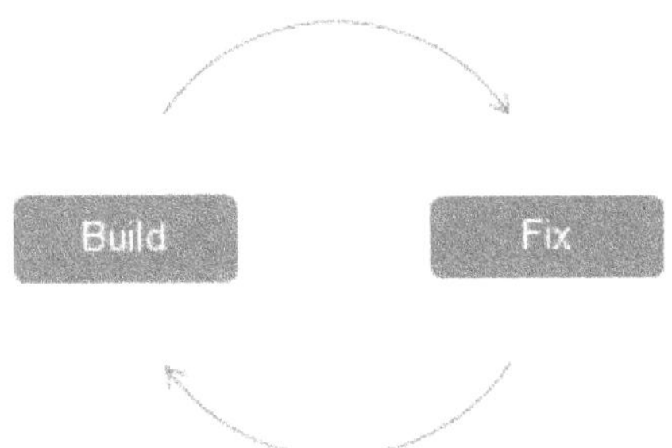

Figure 4: Build and Fix Model

1.8.2   WATERFALL MODEL

The **Waterfall Model** is a **linear and sequential** software development model. It divides the project into a set of distinct phases and assumes that:

- All major **requirements can be identified early**.
- Each phase is **completed before moving** to the next.
- There is limited feedback between phases.

Because of its structured nature, the waterfall model is:
- Easy to understand and explain.
- Suitable for projects where requirements are relatively **stable and well-defined**

1.8.2.1 Classical Waterfall Model

The **Classical Waterfall Model** is one of the earliest and most straightforward process models. It follows a strict, linear sequence of phases, assuming that **no major changes** will occur after a phase is completed. Most other traditional life cycle models have evolved by relaxing or extending this basic pattern.

As shown in **Figure 5**, the classical waterfall divides the software development process into the following six phases, with almost no iteration or feedback between them:

1. Feasibility Study

- Objective: Determine whether the proposed project is **practical and worthwhile**.

- Activities:
    - Technical feasibility analysis
    - Economic and financial feasibility
    - Operational feasibility

- Output: A **feasibility report** recommending whether to proceed, modify, or abandon the project.

2. Analysis

- Objective: Understand and document **what** the system must do.

- Activities:
    - Detailed study of user needs and environment
    - Requirements elicitation and modeling

- Output: A well-defined **Software Requirements Specification (SRS)** document.

3. Design

- Objective: Decide **how** the system will meet the requirements.

- Activities:
    - High-level (architectural) design: modules, interfaces, data flow
    - Detailed design: algorithms, data structures, database schema

- Output: **Design documents** that serve as a blueprint for implementation.

4. Implementation

- Objective: Translate design into working code.

- Activities:
    - Coding of modules according to design specifications
    - Unit testing of individual modules to check for local correctness

- Output: **Source code** and **unit test results**.

5. Integration and System Testing

- Objective: Combine all modules into a complete system and verify that it works as intended.

- Activities:
    - Integration of modules
    - System testing against the SRS (functional, performance, reliability tests, etc.)

- Output:
    - An integrated **software system**
    - **Test plan** and **test reports** documenting the testing activities and results

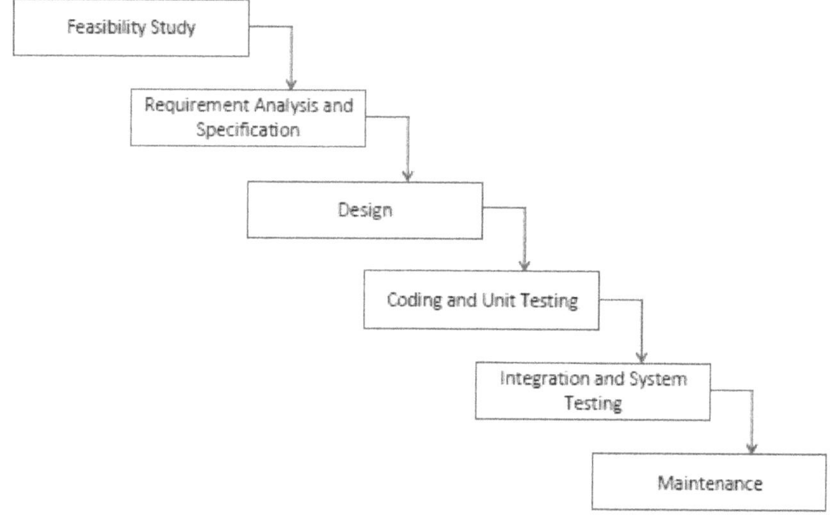

Figure 5: Classical waterfall model

6. Operation and Maintenance

- Objective: Deploy the system to users and keep it operational over time.

- Activities:
    - Installation and configuration
    - Ongoing maintenance (corrections, adaptations, enhancements)

- Output:
  - Operational system
  - **User manuals**, administration guides, and updated documentation.

Strengths of the Waterfall Model

- **Simple and easy to understand**
  The linear structure makes it straightforward to teach, learn, and manage, especially in environments that prefer formal documentation.
- **Clear phase boundaries**
  Each phase has a well-defined set of activities and deliverables, which supports planning, monitoring, and control.
- **Good for stable requirements**
  When requirements are unlikely to change, the upfront specification and design can be effective.
- **Early estimation of cost and schedule**
  Because all phases and deliverables are defined early, it is easier to estimate **budget, timelines, and resource needs**, which can help manage client expectations.

Weaknesses

- **Late discovery of serious errors**
  The software is typically not available for user evaluation or real testing until near the end of the project. Major requirement misunderstandings or design flaws may surface very late, making them costly to fix.
- **Poor handling of changing requirements**
  The model assumes requirements are stable and complete at the start. In reality, requirements often evolve during development, making strict waterfall difficult and expensive to apply.
- **Limited feedback and iteration**

The classical version has no explicit feedback loops between phases. If an error is found in a later phase, going back to earlier phases is not naturally supported by the model.

Because of these limitations, the **pure classical waterfall** is rarely followed in modern practice. Instead, variations with feedback and incremental delivery, or more flexible models (like iterative, incremental, and agile approaches), are preferred for most real-world projects.

1.8.2.2 *Iterative Waterfall Model*

The **Iterative Waterfall Model** is a refinement of the Classical Waterfall Model, introduced to address its rigid, one-way flow. In this version, **review and feedback points** are added between major phases.

If a problem is discovered during a later phase (e.g., during design or testing), the team is allowed to **"go back"** to an earlier phase through controlled **return paths** or **feedback loops**. This makes the model somewhat more flexible and realistic than the pure classical waterfall.

Strengths

> - **More practical than Classical Waterfall**
>   Feedback between phases allows the team to detect and correct errors **earlier**, rather than waiting until the end.
> - **Lower cost of fixing early defects**
>   Since issues can be identified and corrected in earlier stages, the **cost of rework** is generally lower than in the classical model where problems are often discovered late.

Weaknesses

> - **Limited risk management**
>
>   Although better than the classical model, the iterative waterfall still does **not explicitly handle risk** (technical

risk, requirement volatility, etc.) as effectively as Spiral or Agile models.

> **Rigid phase structure**

The model still follows a mostly **fixed sequence of phases**, which can limit productivity and flexibility in projects where requirements change frequently.

> **More suitable for smaller, well-understood projects**
The iterative waterfall works best when the problem domain is **well understood** and the project size is **moderate**. It is not ideal for very large, complex, or highly uncertain projects.

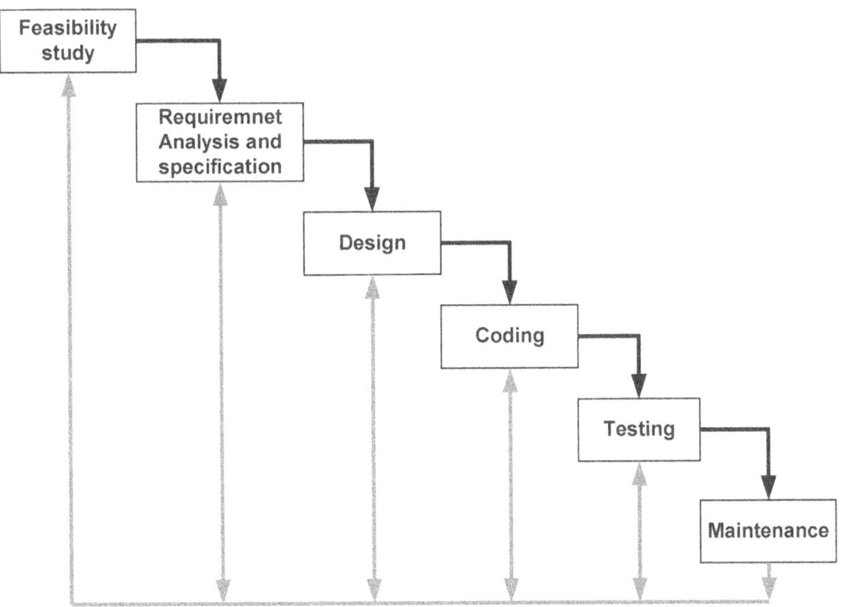

Figure 6: Iterative Waterfall Model

When to Use the Waterfall Model

The Waterfall Model is best suited for software development projects that have:

- ➤ well-defined and stable requirements
- ➤ well-defined and rigid timeline
- ➤ Limited and clearly scoped functionality
- ➤ A low degree of complexity
- ➤ Well-established processes and procedures
- ➤ Reengineering or porting of existing systems

1.8.3   PROTOTYPING MODEL

The **Prototyping Model** focuses on building a **working model (prototype)** of the software early in the development process. This prototype:

- Implements **partial functionality**.

- May **not** have complete logic, performance tuning, or robust error handling.

- Is primarily used to **clarify and refine requirements**.

The main purpose of prototyping is to **reduce uncertainty** in requirements and design. Users can **see and interact** with a preliminary version of the system and provide feedback before full-scale development begins. This helps:

- Ensure that **customer requirements are correctly understood**.

- Allow users to **experiment with proposed features and interfaces**.

- Reduce the risk of building the "wrong" system.

Main Steps in the Prototyping Model

1. **Requirements Identification**

    o Focuses on understanding the **basic product requirements**, especially the **user interface** and main workflows.

- o Internal design details and non-functional aspects (performance, security, scalability) may be temporarily simplified or postponed.

2. **Quick Design**

- o A **rough, high-level design** is created based on the initial requirements.

- o Emphasis is on layout, screens, menus, and basic navigation rather than detailed internals.

3. **Develop Initial Prototype**

- o A working prototype is constructed to **demonstrate the main features and user interface**.

- o The goal is to provide an approximate **"look and feel"** of the final product.

4. **Customer Evaluation of the Prototype**

- o The prototype is shown to customers and key stakeholders.

- o They interact with it and provide **structured feedback** about functionality, usability, and missing features.

5. **Review, Revise, and Enhance Prototype**

- o Developers analyze feedback and assess the **feasibility** of requested changes in terms of time, cost, and technology.

- o Some requirements may be **negotiated** or re-prioritized if they are unrealistic or outside constraints.

- o Agreed changes are incorporated, improving the prototype iteratively until the requirements are stable enough to proceed to full-scale development.

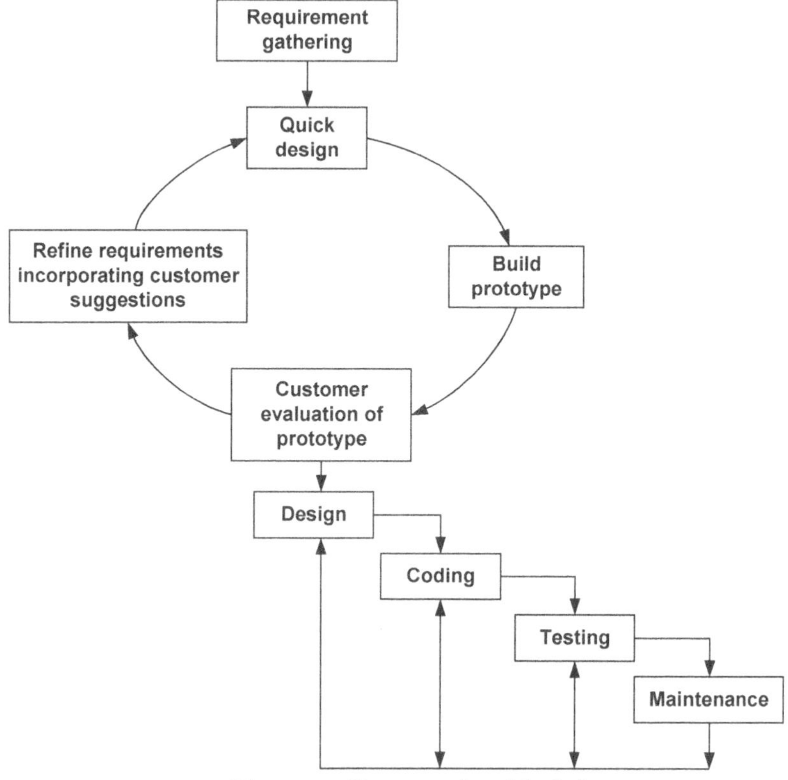

Figure 7: Prototyping Model

Horizontal and Vertical Prototypes

Prototypes can be viewed along two dimensions:

- **Horizontal Prototype**

  - o Provides a **broad view of the system**, focusing on the **user interface and major screens**.

  - o Covers many features at a **shallow** level (no full internal logic).

- o Useful for demonstrating **overall navigation, layout, and user experience**.

- **Vertical Prototype**

  - o Focuses deeply on **one specific feature or subsystem**.

  - o Implements detailed functionality, including **database operations, processing logic, and interactions** for that part.

  - o Useful for analyzing **technical feasibility, performance, and integration** of critical subsystems.

1.8.3.1 *Types of Software Prototyping*

Several prototyping approaches are used in practice, each suitable for different situations. Common types include:

1. Throwaway (Rapid) Prototyping

- A quick prototype is built with **minimal requirement analysis and design**.
- The aim is to **explore and clarify user requirements** rapidly.
- After requirements are better understood, the prototype is **discarded** ("thrown away").
- The **final system is then developed from scratch** using the refined requirements.

Useful when initial requirements are very **uncertain** and you just need to learn what the user really wants.

2. Evolutionary Prototyping

- A functional prototype is built with limited features and then **gradually extended and refined**.

- The prototype is **not discarded**; it evolves into the **final system** through multiple iterations.
- New requirements are incorporated as they become clearer.

Useful when requirements are expected to **change continuously** and the system needs to be delivered in stages.

3. Incremental Prototyping

- Multiple **partial prototypes** are developed for **different subsystems or features**.
- Each prototype is tested and refined independently.
- Finally, all these subsystems are **integrated** to form a complete system.

Useful for large systems that can be naturally divided into **independent modules** or services.

4. Extreme Prototyping

Extreme Prototyping is mainly used for **web applications** where the **user interface and user experience (UI/UX)** are very important and requirements are likely to change.

It is usually carried out in **three stages**:

1. **Static Mockups**

    - Simple, non-functional wireframes or page sketches are created.
    - Used to agree on layout, navigation, and basic screen flow.

2. **Interactive HTML Screens**

    - Wireframes are converted into clickable pages using HTML/CSS/JavaScript.
    - Users can navigate between screens and give feedback on the UI/UX.

3. **Backend Integration**

- o The interactive frontend is connected to real backend services (databases, APIs, business logic).
- o The prototype gradually becomes a fully functional application.

Advantages

- Quick user feedback on UI/UX.
- Reduces risk of building a front end that users dislike.

Challenges

- Can be time-consuming if prototypes become very detailed.
- May encourage frequent change requests (scope creep).

When to Use

- For **web applications** with rich interfaces.
- When **requirements are unclear or evolving**, and user experience is a key success factor.

Note: "Extreme Prototyping" here refers to a **web application prototyping approach**, not to be confused with **Extreme Programming (XP)**.

1.8.4   SPIRAL MODEL

The **Spiral Model**, proposed by **Barry Boehm (1988)**, is a **risk-driven** software process model that combines ideas from the Waterfall Model, Prototyping, and Iterative development. It is often called a **"meta-model"** because other models can be seen as special cases of it.

The process is visualized as a **spiral** with multiple **loops (cycles)**. Each loop represents one phase or level of refinement of the product. As the project progresses, the spiral moves outward, indicating **increasing project scope and cost**.

Each cycle of the spiral typically includes four main activities:

1. **Planning (Objective Setting)**

- o Define objectives for this cycle.

- o Identify alternatives (e.g., different design options, technologies).

- o Note constraints (e.g., cost, schedule, standards, technologies).

2. **Risk Analysis**

- o Evaluate alternatives with respect to objectives and constraints.

- o Identify technical, managerial, and other risks.

- o Plan and (if possible) execute **risk mitigation** actions.

3. **Development (Engineering)**

- o Develop the next version/level of the product.

- o Activities may include prototyping, design, coding, and testing.

- o The depth and detail of development increase with each spiral.

4. **Customer Evaluation (Assessment and Planning)**

- o Present the result of the current cycle (prototype or product increment) to stakeholders.

- o Collect feedback and assess whether goals were met.

- o Plan the next cycle: update objectives, refine requirements, and decide whether to continue, change direction, or stop.

In the spiral diagram:

Starting at the center of the spiral, each development phase (software requirements, product design, detailed design, and implementation) involves one cycle of the spiral. (Aggarwal, 2005)

- The **radial dimension** represents the **cumulative cost** incurred so far.
- The **angular dimension** represents **progress** within each cycle.
- Each loop passes through the four quadrants (Planning → Risk Analysis → Development → Evaluation).

Early (inner) loops may focus on **requirements and prototyping**, while later (outer) loops focus on **detailed design, implementation, and refinement**. As shown by the quadrants in the Figure 8,

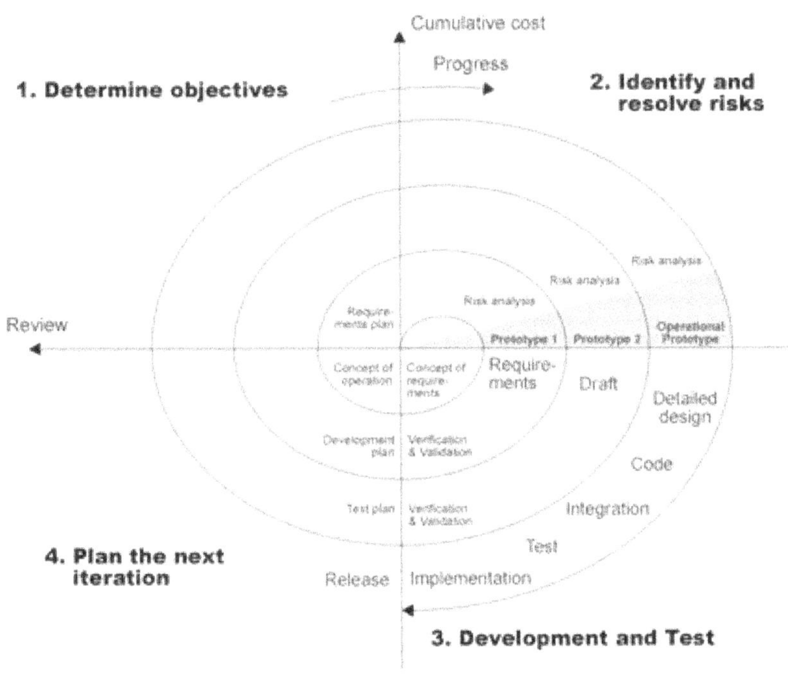

Figure 8: Boehm's Spiral Model (Boehm, 1988)

Risk analysis and the risk-driven approach:

A key idea in the Spiral Model is that **risk drives decisions**. For each cycle:

- Objectives and alternatives are identified first.

- These alternatives are evaluated in terms of **risk** (technical uncertainty, requirement instability, performance doubts, etc.).

- The team chooses the **safest and most promising path**, often using **prototypes, simulations, or experiments** to reduce high risks before committing to full-scale development.

By handling risks early and repeatedly, the Spiral Model aims to **prevent major failures** and reduce costly late-stage surprises.

Strengths of the Spiral Model

- **Combines Best Practices:** Integrates elements from waterfall (structured phases), prototyping (early models), and iterative development (repeated cycles).

- **Iterative and Incremental:** Supports gradual refinement of the system, with each cycle adding detail or functionality.

- **Strong Risk Management:** Each cycle includes structured **risk identification, analysis, and mitigation**, which is critical for complex or high-risk projects.

- **Flexible Use of Prototyping:** Prototypes can be introduced whenever useful to clarify requirements, explore designs, or assess feasibility.

- **Supports Changing Requirements:** Because the process is iterative, user feedback and requirement changes can be incorporated at multiple points.

- **Structured Yet Flexible:** Retains a systematic, phased approach like the waterfall, but with more flexibility for revisiting earlier decisions.

Weaknesses of the Spiral Model

- **Risk of Endless Iteration:** Without clear exit criteria and strong project management, the project may keep cycling without a defined end ("analysis paralysis").

- **Complexity and Overhead:** The model can be **cumbersome** for small projects; formal risk assessments and multiple cycles may introduce unnecessary overhead.

- **Requires Experienced Teams:** Effective risk analysis demands **skilled and experienced engineers and managers**. Poor risk assessment weakens the entire model.

When to Use the Spiral Model

The Spiral Model is particularly suitable when:

- **Cost and Risk Management Are Critical** Projects where **failures are very costly** (e.g., defense, aerospace, critical infrastructure).

- **Medium to High-Risk Projects:** Systems involving new technology, complex integration, or high performance and reliability requirements.

- **User Needs Are Uncertain or Evolving:** Users are unsure of what they want, or major requirement changes are expected during development.

- **Complex and Novel Systems:** Projects with **complex, evolving requirements** or entirely **new product lines** where significant unknowns exist.

For small, low-risk, or very well-understood projects, the overhead of the Spiral Model is usually not justified.

1.8.5   SUCCESSIVE VERSIONS OR INCREMENTAL MODEL

The **Incremental Model** (also called **Successive Versions Model**) develops a system in a series of **increments (versions)** rather than delivering everything at once.

- A **basic working version** with core functionality is built first.

- In subsequent increments, **new features and improvements** are added.

- Over time, the full system is realized as a **combination of all increments**.

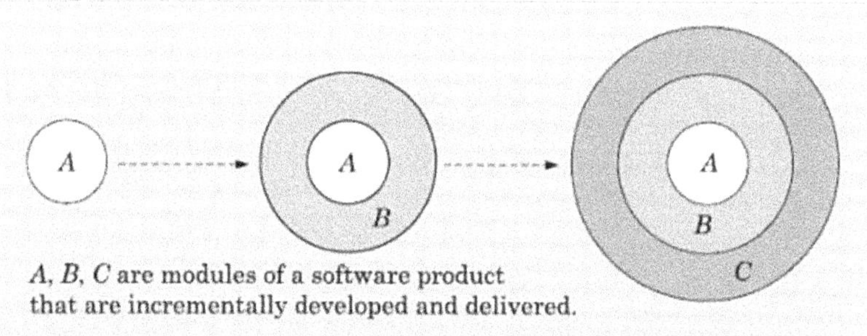

Figure 9: Conceptual view of incremental development

The incremental model is schematically shown in Figure 9. Each increment typically goes through its own mini life cycle (requirements → design → implementation → testing → deployment), often using a mini-waterfall or similar structured approach.

When to Use the Incremental Model

- **Early Use of Core Features Is Needed** Customers want to start using the **most important features early**, instead of waiting for the full product to be finished.

- **Large Projects with Long Schedules** For large systems, delivering in increments makes development **manageable** and allows partial deployment.

- **Most Requirements Are Known but May Evolve** The majority of functionality is known at the start, but some details are expected to **change or grow** over time.

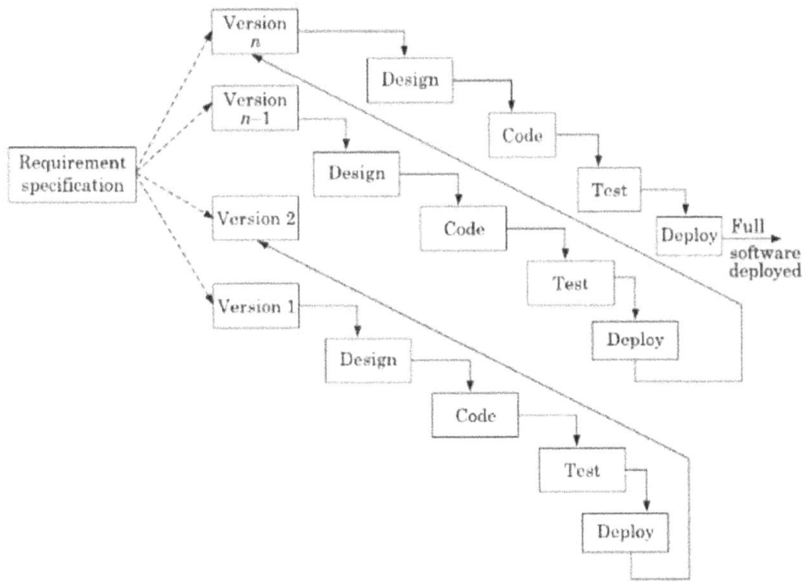

Figure 10: Phases of Incremental Model

Strengths of the Incremental Model

- **Early User Feedback**
  Users can **experiment with a partially developed system** early in the project. Feedback from initial increments can be incorporated into later ones, leading to a system that better matches real needs.

- **Reduced Risk and Easier Testing**
  Core modules are delivered and **tested thoroughly** before later increments are added. Problems can be discovered and fixed early, which lowers technical risk.

- **Better Resource Utilization**
  Development can be planned in **stages**, aligning with budget cycles, staff availability, or market deadlines.

- **Prioritization of Features**
  Critical features can be delivered first, while less essential features can be added later (or even dropped).

Weaknesses of the Incremental Model

- **Difficulty in Dividing the System:** It can be challenging to **split the system** into increments that:

  - Are meaningful and usable by the customer.
  - Can be implemented and tested independently.

- **Requires Good Overall Design and Planning**
  The architecture must be designed from the beginning to **support incremental growth**, or later increments may be difficult to integrate.

- **Potential Integration Issues:** As more increments are added, integration and regression testing become more complex if not managed carefully.

1.8.6   EVOLUTIONARY MODELS

Evolutionary models describe development as a sequence of iterations in which the software is gradually refined and extended. At each iteration, the system moves from one state to another for each software engineering activity (requirements, design, coding, testing, etc.). With every cycle, the product becomes **more complete and more complex**.

In this view, events trigger transitions between states. For example, during early design, if an inconsistency is discovered in the analysis model, an event such as **"analysis model correction"** may be raised. This moves the analysis activity from a state like **"done"** back to **"awaiting changes"**, so that corrections can be made before proceeding.

Unlike the **Incremental Model**, where a relatively complete set of requirements is first captured and documented in the SRS and then implemented in increments, the **Evolutionary Model** assumes that:

- Requirements, plans, and technical solutions **evolve over time**.

- Each iteration may **change or extend** the understanding of the problem and its solution.

This makes evolutionary approaches especially suitable for projects in which:

- Features are **uncertain or unpredictable**, and

- Significant changes are expected during development (for example, in **new product development** or innovation-driven projects). (Mall, 2018).

Evolutionary Model of development is shown in Figure 11

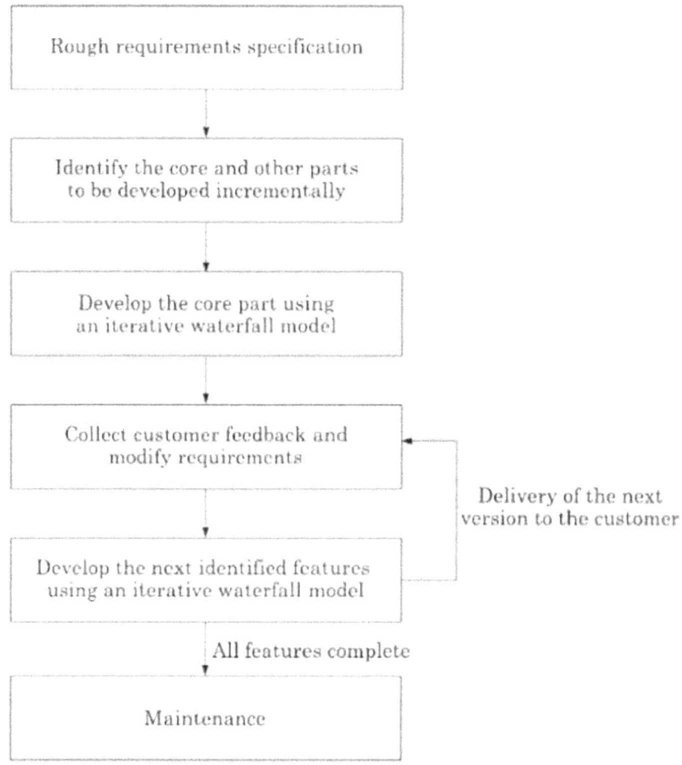

Figure 11: Evolutional Software Process Model

Strengths

- **Accurate Requirement Elicitation:** Users are able to interact with a **partially developed system** early in the project. Their feedback helps refine and correct requirements, which significantly reduces the number of change requests after the full system is delivered.

- **Flexible Handling of Change:** Because no rigid long-term plan is fixed from the beginning, change requests can be handled more easily. The rework caused by changes is usually smaller than in strict waterfall-style models.

Weaknesses

- **Difficulty in Decomposing Features:** For small projects, it may be hard to split the required functionality into meaningful pieces that can be separately developed and delivered. Even in larger systems, features may be tightly coupled, making incremental planning and delivery challenging.

- **Risk of Ad Hoc Design:** As design decisions are taken and revised incrementally, there is a danger that the overall architecture becomes **ad hoc**, with insufficient attention to maintainability, performance, or optimal structure. For medium-sized projects with clear requirements, an **iterative waterfall** or similar structured model may be a better fit.

1.8.7   V-SHAPED MODEL

The **V-Shaped Model (V-Model)** is a refinement of the Waterfall Model that explicitly emphasizes **verification and validation (V&V)** at each stage of development. It is particularly suitable for systems that require **high reliability** (for example, healthcare, avionics, or safety-critical control systems) where most requirements are known before development begins.

Instead of proceeding purely linearly, the model is shaped like a "V":

- The **left side** of the V represents **verification phases** (requirements and design activities).

- The **bottom** represents **coding/implementation**.

- The **right side** represents **validation phases** (various levels of testing).

For each development phase on the left, there is a **corresponding test phase** on the right. Test planning and test design therefore begin **in parallel** with their related specification activities, rather than being postponed until after coding

This early planning:

- Encourages **clear, testable requirements and designs**.

- Can save significant time and effort by detecting issues before implementation.

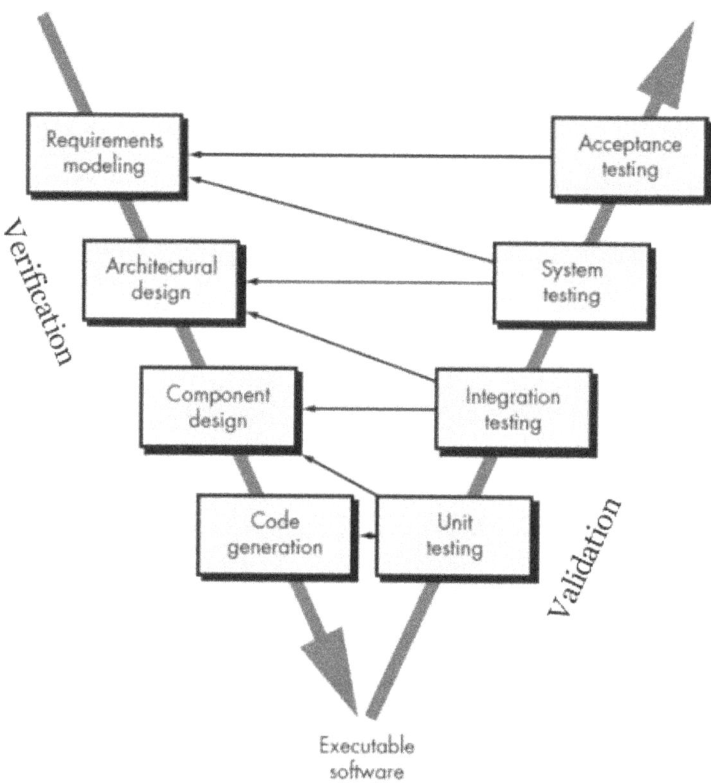

Figure 12: V-Shaped Model (Pressman, 2005)

1.8.7.1 *Verification Phases (Left Side of the "V")*

These phases focus on defining and refining **what the system should do** and **how it should be structured**.

(a) Requirements Analysis

- Objective: Understand **what the ideal system should accomplish** from the users' and stakeholders' point of view.

- Activities:

  - Elicit and analyze user needs.
  - Document requirements in a **User Requirements or SRS document**.

- Output: A logical description of system behavior, independent of implementation details.

Corresponding test activity (right side): **User Acceptance Testing (UAT)**.

(b) System Design

- Objective: Decide how to realize all user requirements at the **system level**.

- Activities:

  - Study the requirements document and analyze feasibility.
  - Propose and refine system-level solutions.
  - Negotiate changes if some requirements are not feasible.

- Output: **System design specifications**, describing overall system structure and major components.

Corresponding test activity: **System Testing** (does the integrated system meet the system design/specification?).

(c) Architecture Design (High-Level Design)

- Objective: Define the **software architecture** that best satisfies the system requirements.

- Activities:

- o Identify major modules/services and their responsibilities.
- o Specify interfaces and dependencies between modules.
- o Prepare architectural diagrams and choose architectural patterns.
- o Plan **integration testing strategy** (how components will be combined and tested).

Corresponding test activity: **Integration Testing** (checking interfaces and interactions between modules).

(d) Module or Component Design (Low-Level Design)

- Objective: Design each module or component in sufficient detail for coding.

- Activities:

  - o Define internal data structures, algorithms, and control flow.
  - o Specify detailed interfaces (parameters, return types, error handling).
  - o Design **unit test cases** for each module.

Corresponding test activity: **Unit Testing** (verifying each component individually).

1.8.7.2 Validation Phases (Right Side of the "V")

Validation phases check whether the software built during coding **meets its specifications** and **satisfies user needs**. Each corresponds to a verification phase on the left.

(a) Unit Testing

- Verifies the correctness of **individual modules or components** against their low-level design.

- Typically performed by developers, often using white-box techniques.

- Fixing defects at this stage is far cheaper than discovering them after deployment.

(b) Integration Testing

- Tests how modules **work together** once they are combined.

- Focuses on **interfaces, data flow, and interactions** between integrated components.

- Often uses black-box techniques, as the main concern is behavior at module boundaries.

(c) System Testing

- Compares the **integrated system** against the **system design and SRS**.
- Verifies functional and non-functional requirements (performance, reliability, security, etc.).
- Confirms that the system, as a whole, behaves as specified.

(d) User Acceptance Testing (UAT)

- Validates the system against **user requirements** defined in the requirements analysis phase.
- Performed by users or customer representatives.
- Determines whether the system is **acceptable for deployment** or whether further changes are needed.

Strengths of the V-Shaped Model

- **Early V&V Planning:** Verification and validation activities are planned from the start, not left as an afterthought. Every deliverable must be **testable**.

- **Clear Milestones and Traceability:** Each phase has clear inputs and outputs, making it easier for project management to **track progress by milestones** and maintain traceability from requirements to tests.

- **Ease of Use:** The model is conceptually simple and works well when **requirements are stable and fully known** at the outset.

Weaknesses of the V-Shaped Model

- **Limited Support for Iteration and Change:** The model does not naturally support **iterative development** or frequent requirement changes. Changes late in the process can be expensive.

- **Poor Handling of Concurrency:** It does not easily model concurrent activities or overlapping phases, which are common in modern development practices.

- **No Built-in Risk Management:** The V-Model does not explicitly address **risk analysis**, which can be a serious limitation for high-risk or innovative projects.

When to use the V-Shape

- The system requires **high reliability** (e.g., medical, aerospace, safety-critical or regulatory environments).

- **All major requirements are known up front**, and significant changes are unlikely.

- The solution approach and technology are **well understood and established**.

- The model can be **slightly adapted** to handle moderate changes after the analysis phase (e.g. via controlled change management).

For highly dynamic, or high-risk projects, more flexible iterative or agile models are often preferable.

1.9 SELECTION OF A LIFE CYCLE MODEL

Choosing an appropriate **software life cycle model** is a critical project decision. The chosen model influences project cost, schedule, quality, and even the probability of success. No single model is best for all projects; **the choice depends on several factors**.

- **Nature of Requirements**

  - Are requirements clear and stable, or vague and likely to change?
  - Are they well-documented, or still evolving through user discussion and prototyping?

- **Experience and Technical Knowledge of the Development Team**

  - Is the team familiar with the domain and technology stack?
  - Do they have experience with iterative, agile, or risk-driven models?

- **User Involvement**

  - How frequently can users or domain experts participate?
  - Is continuous feedback available, or only limited interaction (e.g., at milestones)?

- **Type of Project**

  - Completely **new system** or **enhancement/port** of an existing product?
  - Maintenance and extension often suit incremental or evolutionary approaches.

- **Project Schedule**

- o Is the timeline **tight** and fixed, or relatively **flexible**?
- o Are staged deliveries or early partial releases needed?

- **Budget Constraints**
  - o Is the budget fixed and limited, or can it expand based on results and feedback?

- **Risk Level**
  - o What are the **technical, financial, and operational risks**?
  - o High-risk projects often benefit from **risk-driven models** such as the **Spiral Model**, which support early risk identification, analysis, and mitigation.

Examples of Model Selection

- **Waterfall Model is** Appropriate when:

  - o Requirements are **well understood and stable** from the start.
  - o Development team is experienced with the technology and domain.
  - o **User participation** is limited after the requirements phase.
  - o Funding is **stable**, and the organization prefers formal documentation and milestone-based management.

- **Evolutionary Models are** Suitable when:

  - o The system is **relatively complex**, but requirements do **not change very frequently**.
  - o Some **user feedback** is needed, but continuous end-user involvement is not practical.
  - o The development team is **new to the technology** and needs to learn and refine through iterations, possibly with initial domain training.

Table 1: Comparison of Incremental, Spiral, Prototyping and V-Model

Aspect	Increment al Model	Spiral Model	Prototyping Model	V-Model (V-Shaped)
Core Idea	System delivered in a series of increments (versions); each increment adds more functionality	Risk-driven iterative cycles: each loop = objectives → risk analysis → development → evaluation.	Build a partial prototype (throwaway or evolving) to clarify requirements before full development.	Extension of waterfall: each development phase has a correspondin g test phase (verification ↔ validation).
Requiremen ts Situation	Most major requirement s known early; some details may evolve over time.	Requiremen ts unclear, evolving, or with many unknowns.	Requirements poorly understood; users are unsure what they want.	Requirement s stable and well defined from the beginning.
Risk Handling	Medium – each increment reduces risk by delivering and testing part of the system.	Strong, explicit risk analysis in every cycle; risk is the main driver.	Reduces requirement/usabili ty risk through early user experimentation.	Limited explicit risk handling; emphasis is on systematic testing, not risk analysis.
User Involvement	Periodic feedback at the end of each increment.	Regular customer evaluation at the end of each spiral cycle.	High, especially during prototype evaluation and refinement.	Mainly at the requirements phase and during User Acceptance Testing; not continuous.
Typical Use / Suitability	Large systems where core features are needed early, and the system can be logically split into increments.	Medium to high-risk, complex or innovative projects; new product lines.	UI-intensive systems, new concepts, or projects where requirement clarification is the primary goal.	Safety-critical or high-reliability systems (e.g. medical, aerospace) needing strong documentatio n and formal testing.

1.10 SOFTWARE QUALITY STANDARDS: AN OVERVIEW

1.10.1 SOFTWARE QUALITY

Software quality refers to the degree to which a software program meets its specified requirements and is free from defects, errors, and other malfunctions.

Quality includes multiple attributes, such as:

- **Functionality** – Does the software provide the required features?

- **Reliability** – Does it perform consistently without failure?

- **Usability** – Is it easy to learn and operate?

- **Performance** – Does it respond and process within acceptable time and resource limits?

- **Security** – Does it protect data and resist unauthorized access or attacks?

High-quality software is therefore **effective, efficient, and user-friendly**, fulfilling its intended purpose without causing unintended side effects. Achieving such quality requires:

- Systematic **testing and verification**

- **Reviews and inspections**

- **Measurement and continuous improvement** throughout the software development life cycle.

1.10.2 SOFTWARE QUALITY STANDARDS

Software quality standards are formal documents that define **principles, practices, and criteria** for developing and maintaining high-quality software. They:

- Provide **benchmarks** for process and product quality.

- Help organizations ensure that software solutions **consistently satisfy user and stakeholder requirements**.

- Support **certification, assessment, and comparison** between organizations.

In this section we focus on three important frameworks related to software processes and quality:

1. **Capability Maturity Model (CMM)** by the **Software Engineering Institute (SEI)**.

2. **Malcolm Baldrige National Quality Award** framework.

3. **ISO 9000** family of standards.

1.10.3 SEI-CMM

The **Capability Maturity Model for Software (CMM)** was introduced by the **Software Engineering Institute (SEI)** in 1991 as a major contribution to **software process management and improvement**.

Key points:

- CMM defines **five maturity levels** of software process capability.

- It is **independent of any specific life cycle model**; organizations can apply CMM improvements whether they use waterfall, incremental, spiral, or agile processes.

- Each maturity level provides a **foundation for continuous process improvement**. (Paulk et al., 1991).

(CMM has now been superseded in practice by CMMI, but the five-level structure remains the same

1.10.3.1 The Five Maturity Levels

The levels describe how disciplined and predictable an organization's software processes are. Each level builds on the strengths of the previous one.

Five maturity levels highlight the primary process changes made at each level as shown in Figure 13

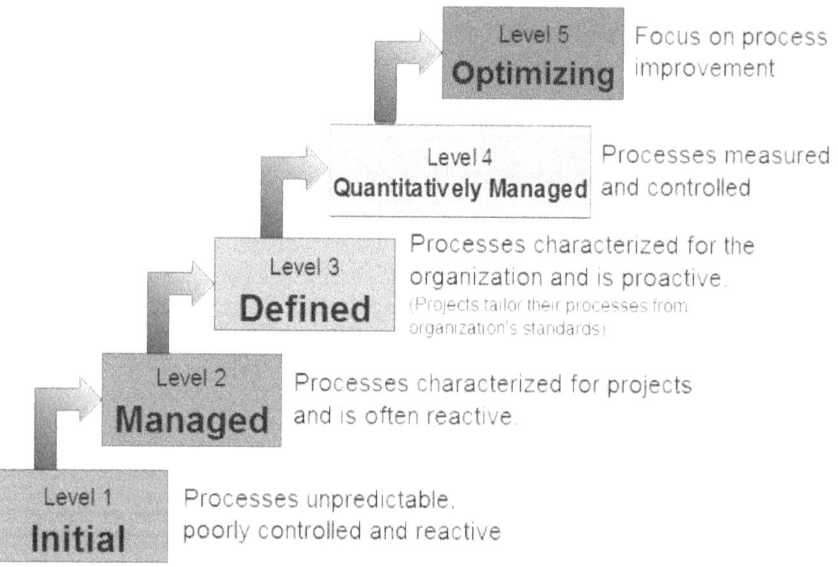

Figure 13: Five CMM Levels

Level 1 – Initial (Ad hoc Process)

- Processes are **ad hoc and disorganized**.

- Few activities are formally defined or documented.

- Project success heavily depends on the **individual skills and heroic efforts** of developers.

- Poor planning and lack of engineering discipline lead to **frequent schedule and cost overruns**.

- Projects tend to be **reactive**, dealing with crises rather than following a controlled plan.

Level 2 – Repeatable (Basic Project Management)

- Basic project management practices are introduced to **track cost, schedule, and functionality**.
- Previous project successes can be **repeated** for similar applications because fundamental management controls are in place.
- Process discipline is still limited but sufficient to **stabilize** projects of similar type.

Level 3 – Defined

- The organization's software processes are **documented, standardized, and integrated** across projects.

- Both **management and engineering activities** follow an approved, tailored version of the organization's standard process.

- This level marks a major shift: software development is now driven by **well-defined processes**, not just by individual project practices.

Level 4 – Managed

- The organization **collects detailed metrics** on both the software process and the resulting products.

- Quantitative techniques are used to **measure, analyze, and control** process performance and product quality.

- The emphasis is on **defect prevention and variability reduction**, moving towards predictable performance.

Level 5 – Optimizing

- Focus is on **continuous process improvement**.

- Quantitative feedback from Level 4, along with **research and experimentation with new technologies**, is used to refine processes.

- Mechanisms are in place to **identify weaknesses proactively** and introduce changes aimed at defect prevention and innovation.

Many Indian multinational companies such as **Infosys, TCS, Wipro Technologies, and HCL Technologies** have achieved **CMM Level 5**, indicating the highest level of process maturity and a strong culture of continuous improvement.

1.10.3.2 Key Process Areas (KPAs)

Except for Level 1, each maturity level is characterized by several **Key Process Areas (KPAs)**. Each KPA groups related activities that, when implemented together, help organizations achieve the goals of that maturity level. They act as **targets** for organizations aspiring to move to a higher level.

- **Level 2 KPAs – Basic Project Management Controls**
  - Requirements Management
  - Software Project Planning

- o Software Project Tracking and Oversight
- o Software Subcontract Management
- o Software Quality Assurance
- o Software Configuration Management

- **Level 3 KPAs – Organization-wide Standardization**

  - o Organization Process Focus
  - o Organization Process Definition
  - o Training Program
  - o Integrated Software Management
  - o Software Product Engineering
  - o Intergroup Coordination
  - o Peer Reviews

- **Level 4 KPAs – Quantitative Management**

  - o Quantitative Process Management
  - o Software Quality Management

- **Level 5 KPAs – Continuous Improvement**

  - o Defect Prevention
  - o Technology Change Management
  - o Process Change Management

Together, these KPAs provide a **roadmap for process improvement**, helping organizations move from informal, unpredictable practices to **disciplined, measurable, and continuously improving software processes**.

1.10.4 MALCOLM BALDRIGE ASSESSMENT

The **Malcolm Baldrige National Quality Award (MBNQA)** is often described as one of the most prestigious quality awards in the United States. The associated **Criteria for Performance Excellence** provide a broad framework for assessing and improving overall organizational performance, not just product quality. (Botten, 1994).

The criteria are organized into the following **seven Categories** (see Figure 14):

1. **Leadership**
Examines how senior leaders set direction, communicate values, and sustain the organization's mission, including governance, ethics, and social responsibility.

2. **Strategic Planning**

Focuses on how the organization develops strategic objectives and action plans, deploys them, and reviews progress.

3. **Customer Focus**

Assesses how the organization engages customers for long-term success and builds a strong customer-focused culture, including listening and complaint-handling processes.

4. **Measurement, Analysis, and Knowledge Management**
Evaluates how the organization selects, gathers, analyzes, manages, and improves data, information, and knowledge to support decision-making and innovation.

5. **Workforce Focus**

Reviews how the organization engages, manages, and develops its workforce to align with mission, strategy, and action plans.

6. **Process Management**

Looks at how key work processes are designed, managed, and continuously improved to deliver value to customers and achieve organizational objectives.

7. **Results**
Reviews performance and improvement in key outcome areas, including:

- o Product and service results

- o Customer-focused results
- o Financial and market results
- o Workforce results
- o Process effectiveness results
- o Leadership and governance results

For software organizations, the Baldrige framework complements software-specific models (such as SEI–CMM/CMMI) by providing a **holistic view of organizational excellence** beyond just engineering processes.

Figure 14: Criteria for Performance excellence framework

1.10.5 INTERNATIONAL ORGANIZATION FOR STANDARDIZATION (ISO)

The **International Organization for Standardization (ISO)** is a global federation of national standards bodies from around 160 countries. Founded in 1947, ISO is a non-governmental organization that develops **international standards** to improve the quality, safety, and efficiency of products and services across industries.

In software engineering, the most relevant documents are the **ISO 9000 family of quality management standards**, which define how organizations should manage and improve their processes to consistently meet customer and regulatory requirements.

1.10.5.1 ISO 9000 Family

The **ISO 9000 family** is a set of standards dealing with **quality management systems (QMS)**. The main standards are:

- **ISO 9000 – Quality Management Systems – Fundamentals and Vocabulary**

    o Defines the basic concepts and terminology used in quality management.

- **ISO 9001 – Quality Management Systems – Requirements**

    o Specifies the requirements an organization must meet to establish, implement, maintain, and continually improve a QMS.

    o It is the **only standard in the family used for certification**.

- **ISO 9004 – Quality Management – Guidelines for Performance Improvement**

    o Provides guidance for organizations that want to go beyond ISO 9001 compliance and improve overall performance and long-term sustainability.

These are **process standards**, not product standards: they do not define how a specific software product should behave, but how **organizational processes** should be managed and controlled.

For software organizations, additional guidance is provided by **ISO/IEC 90003**, which explains how to apply ISO 9001 to **software development, supply, and maintenance**.

1.10.5.2 ISO 9001 and Software

ISO 9001 is the internationally recognized standard for **quality management systems**. When applied to software, ISO 9001 requires that an organization:

- **Plans and controls** key processes such as requirements management, design, coding, testing, release, and maintenance.

- Maintains **documented procedures** and clearly defined responsibilities.

- **Monitors and reviews** process performance using audits, inspections, and management reviews.

- Takes **corrective and preventive actions** when problems occur and uses feedback for continual improvement.

ISO 9001 is **industry-agnostic**, so software organizations typically use it **together with** software-specific models (e.g., SEI–CMM/CMMI):

- ISO 9001 provides a **generic, auditable QMS framework**.

- CMM/CMMI adds **software-engineering-specific practices and maturity levels**.

1.10.5.3 The benefits of implementing ISO 9001

Implementing a QMS based on ISO 9001 can offer several benefits to software organizations:

- **Greater Consistency and Predictability**
  Standardized processes reduce variability in how projects are executed.

- **Reduced Errors and Rework**
  Defined procedures, reviews, and corrective actions help prevent recurring defects and implementation mistakes.

- **Better Resource Utilization and Cost Savings**
  Fewer defects and clearer workflows lead to more efficient use of time, people, and infrastructure.

- **Improved Customer Satisfaction**
  Products and services are delivered more reliably, in line with agreed requirements and schedules.

- **Enhanced Market Credibility**
  ISO 9001 certification is widely recognized as evidence of disciplined and well-managed processes, which can be important for winning contracts, especially in global markets.

1.10.6 RELATIONSHIP AND DIFFERENCE BETWEEN SEI-CMM AND ISO

Both the **Capability Maturity Model (CMM)** and the **ISO 9000/ISO 9001** standards address **quality and process management**, but they do so from different perspectives and with different primary goals.

- **SEI–CMM (and CMMI for Software)**

  - Designed specifically for **software development and maintenance**.

  - Focuses on **internal process capability and maturity**, describing a path from ad hoc practices (Level 1) to optimizing processes (Level 5).

- o Emphasizes **continuous improvement** and the use of metrics to understand and control software processes.

- **ISO 9001**

  - o Generic standard applicable to **all types of organizations and industries**.

  - o Focuses on establishing and maintaining a **documented, auditable quality management system**.

  - o Emphasizes **repeatability, consistency, and conformance** to defined procedures through external audits.

In summary:

- **ISO 9001** provides a **broad, cross-industry QMS framework** and external certification.

- **SEI–CMM** provides a **software-specific maturity model** emphasizing internal capability and continuous improvement.

Many mature software organizations adopt **both**: ISO 9001 for general quality management and market recognition, and CMM/CMMI for **deep software process improvement**

1.10.6.1 Mapping ISO 9001 to the CMM

Although ISO 9001 and CMM use different structures (clauses vs maturity levels and KPAs), they overlap significantly in their expectations for **documented, managed, and improving processes**. The table below gives a simplified thematic mapping

Table 2: Summary Mapping of ISO 9001 Focus Areas to CMM Practices

ISO 9001 Focus Area	Typical ISO 9001 Elements	Closely Related CMM Practices / KPAs
Management Responsibility & Quality Policy	Management commitment, defined responsibilities, quality objectives, management review.	Software Project Planning (SPP), Software Quality Assurance (SQA), Organization Process Focus.
Documented Quality System & Procedures	Documented QMS, procedures, controlled documentation.	SPP, Software Configuration Management (SCM), Organization Process Definition.
Contract & Requirements Management	Contract review, clarification of customer requirements, feasibility assessment.	Requirements Management (RM), SPP, Integrated Software Management.
Design & Development Control	Planning, review, verification, and validation of design work.	Software Product Engineering (SPE), Peer Reviews, SQA.
Purchasing & Supplier/Subcontract Control	Control of purchased products and subcontracted work.	Software Subcontract Management, Integrated Software Management.
Process Control & Production	Defined, planned, and controlled operational processes.	SPP, SPE, Quantitative Process Management (higher maturity levels).
Inspection, Testing & Measuring	Inspection and testing activities; test records; control of measuring equipment.	SPE (testing practices), Peer Reviews, Software Quality Management.
Nonconformity, Corrective Action & Records	Control of nonconforming product, corrective actions, quality records.	SQA, SCM, Defect Prevention, Process Change Management.
Audits & Training	Internal quality audits, training needs and records.	SQA, Training Program (Level 3), Organization Process Focus, measurement and analysis activities.

This mapping illustrates that:

- ISO 9001 can be viewed as defining "what" a disciplined organization should have in its QMS.

- CMM provides more detailed guidance on "how" to build and improve software processes to reach higher levels of maturity.

When to Use Each Framework

- **ISO 9001:** Best suited for organizations needing a broad, industry-agnostic quality management system with a focus on external certification.
- **CMM:** Ideal for software organizations seeking a structured path to process improvement and higher maturity levels, with a focus on internal capability enhancement.

1.10.7 CMM AND ISO COMPARISONS, CONTRASTS, AND APPLICABILITY

Both the Capability Maturity Model (CMM) and the ISO 9000/ISO 9001 standards focus on **quality and process management**, but from different angles:

- **ISO 9001 / ISO 9000 family** is **generic and industry-agnostic**, aimed at reducing customer risk by ensuring suppliers have a documented, auditable quality management system.

- **CMM** is **software-specific**, aimed at improving a software organization's **internal process maturity** so it can consistently deliver higher-quality products.

In simple terms:

- **ISO 9001** concentrates on **establishing and maintaining** a stable, repeatable set of quality practices, verified through external audits.

- **CMM** concentrates on **continuous improvement**, moving through maturity levels and refining processes even after reaching the highest level.

In practice, many organizations use **both together**:

- ISO 9001 as a **broad, cross-industry foundation** for quality management and external certification.

- CMM as a **software-focused roadmap** for long-term process enhancement and higher capability.

1.11 EXERCISES

1.1 What is the *software crisis*? Was the Year 2000 (Y2K) problem an example of a software crisis? Justify your answer.

1.2 What are the main causes of the software crisis? Discuss possible approaches to overcome these problems.

1.3 What are software life cycle models? Explain the advantages and limitations of different Software Development Life Cycle (SDLC) models.

1.4 Explain the Spiral Model of software development with the help of a neat schematic diagram. State any **two advantages** and **two disadvantages** of this model.

1.5 Critically compare the **Waterfall Model** and **Evolutionary Models**. Highlight their key similarities and differences.

1.6 Compare the SEI–CMM framework with ISO-based quality models. How do their aims and approaches to software quality differ?

2   SOFTWARE METRICS

'You can't control what you can't measure'
(DeMarco 1998)

As software systems grow in size and complexity, the need for effective measurement becomes increasingly critical. **Software metrics** provide a quantitative foundation for the planning, design, construction, testing, and maintenance of software systems.

They help engineers and managers to:

- Assess the **quality** of software products

- Estimate and manage **effort, cost, and schedule**

- Monitor and improve **process performance**

- Support **data-driven decision-making** throughout the software development life cycle (SDLC) (Bhatia et al., 2010).

This chapter introduces different types of software metrics, their classification, and how they are applied to improve both **software products** and **software processes**. (Bhatia et al., 2010).

This chapter explores the various types of software metrics, their classification, and how they can be applied to improve software development processes and products.

Learning Objectives
After studying this chapter, you should be able to:

- Explain the **importance of software metrics** in software engineering.

- Classify and distinguish between **product, process, and project metrics**.

- Apply **size, design, data structure, and information flow metrics** to real systems.

- Describe and interpret **object-oriented and process metrics**.

- Understand how **software analytics** supports data-driven decision-making in projects.

2.1 CLASSIFICATION OF SOFTWARE METRICS

2.1.1 OVERVIEW

Software metrics are measures that provide insight into the effectiveness of the software development process and the quality of the software product.

They are essential tools for both **project managers** and **developers** to:

- Monitor project and process **progress**

- Assess and control **quality**

- Identify areas for **improvement**

2.1.2 CATEGORIES OF SOFTWARE METRICS

Software metrics can be broadly classified into three main categories:

1. Product Metrics
2. Process Metrics
3. Project Metrics

1. Product Metrics

- Metrics that measure the characteristics of the software product itself.
- Examples:
  - ➤ **Size Metrics**: Lines of Code (LOC), Function Points (FP).
  - ➤ **Complexity Metrics**: Cyclomatic Complexity.
  - ➤ **Quality Metrics**: Defect Density, Mean Time to Failure (MTTF).
  - ➤ **Design Metrics**: Measures related to modularity, coupling, cohesion, etc.
- **Purpose**:
  - ➤ Assess the **quality, structure, and characteristics** of the software product.
  - ➤ Support decisions about **refactoring, testing effort, maintainability, and reliability**.

2. Process Metrics

Metrics that measure the effectiveness and efficiency of the software development process.

- Examples:
  - o **Defect Removal Efficiency (DRE)**: Percentage of defects removed during the process.
  - o **Process Compliance**: Adherence to standards and procedures.
- **Purpose**: Evaluate and improve the software development process to enhance productivity and product quality.

3. Project Metrics

Project metrics characterize the **execution and control** of a software project.

Examples:

- **Schedule Variance (SV)**: Difference between planned and actual progress.

- **Cost Variance (CV)**: Difference between budgeted and actual costs.
- **Resource Utilization**: Efficiency in using resources like personnel and equipment.

Purpose:

> Quantify key aspects such as **cost, schedule, quality, and productivity** at the project level.
> Support **data-driven management** of the project by tracking:

  - Planned vs. actual **effort**
  - **Defect** trends
  - **Requirements stability** and scope changes

> Enable early detection of problems and more informed corrective actions.

In this chapter, our primary focus will be on **product** and **process** metrics. A good understanding of these metrics will help you improve software quality, estimate effort and staffing, and design more efficient and maintainable software systems.

2.2 PRODUCT METRICS

Product metrics focus on the **internal properties** and **quality attributes** of the software. They help to ensure that the final product:

- Meets its **functional and non-functional requirements**

- Is **reliable, maintainable, and efficient**

Some of the most important product metrics are **size metrics**, **complexity metrics**, **quality metrics**, and various **design metrics**

2.2.1   SIZE METRICS

Size metrics quantify the size of the software product, which can be used to estimate effort, time, and resources required for development and maintenance.

One of the oldest and most widely used size metrics is **Lines of Code (LOC)**.

2.2.1.1 *Lines of code*

Lines of Code (LOC) is one of the most widely used metrics for estimating the size of a software project. The LOC metric measures the size of a project based on the number of lines of statements or instructions written in the source code. In this measurement, comments and headers are typically excluded.

Shortcomings of LOC:
- **Difficult to Estimate Early:** Estimating LOC by analyzing the problem specification is challenging. Accurate LOC estimation is often only possible after the code has been fully developed.
- **Variability in Effort:** Two different source files with the same number of lines may not require the same amount of effort. For example, a file with complex logic will generally require more effort than one with simpler logic, making LOC a less reliable metric for estimating effort.
- **Programmer Variability:** LOC can vary significantly between programmers. An experienced developer might write the same logic in fewer lines than a novice, which can skew the accuracy of LOC-based estimations.

Despite these limitations, LOC remains a **useful and widely collected metric** because:

- It is **easy to compute** (often automated by tools).

- Historical LOC data can support **rough effort and cost estimation** for similar future projects.

2.2.1.2 *Function point metrics*

Function Point (FP) metrics address many limitations of Lines of Code (LOC) by measuring **what the software does** for the user, rather than **how it is coded**. LOC depends on language, coding style, and implementation choices; Function Points are based on **user-visible functionality**, so they are more stable and easier to estimate early.

The basic idea of **Function Point Analysis (FPA)** is:

The size of a software project is directly related to the **number** and **complexity** of the functions it provides to its users.

This makes function points especially useful during **project planning**, when only the **problem specification** is available.

Objectives of Function Point Analysis (FPA)-

- **Measure user-requested functionality**

  Quantify the amount of functionality the user *requests and receives*, independent of the technology used.

- **Measure development and maintenance independent of technology**

  Provide a metric that does not depend on programming language, tools, or hardware platform.

- **Minimize measurement overhead**

  Be simple enough that measurement does not impose excessive effort on the development team.

- **Provide consistent, comparable measures**

  Standardize the measurement of functionality so that different projects and organizations can be compared more reliably.

Types of Function Points in FPA

1. Transactional Functional Type –

These represent **processing functions** that involve input, output, or inquiry by the user:

a) **External Input (EI)**
   Processes data or control information entering the system from outside its boundary. e.g., user input forms, data entry screens.
b) **External Output (EO)**
   Sends data or control information from inside the system to an external destination. e.g., reports, messages, generated documents.
c) **External Inquiry (EQ)**
   A combination of input and output that retrieves data without significant internal processing. e.g., Query screens that display customer details on request.

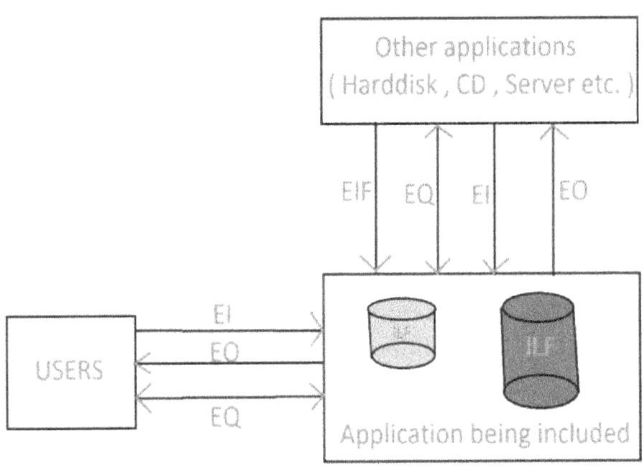

Figure 15: Function Point Analysis (illustrates the relationships between different functional types)

2. Data Functional Type –

These represent **logical data groups** maintained or referenced by the application:

a) Internal Logical File (ILF): A user identifiable group of logically related data or control information maintained within the boundary of the application.

b) External Interface File (EIF): A group of user recognizable logically related data allusion to the software but maintained within the boundary of another software. e.g., product catalogue file owned by another system but read by this system.

Function Point Calculation

Function Points are computed by:

1. **Counting and classifying all functions**

   o   Identify all EIs, EOs, EQs, ILFs, and EIFs.

   o   Classify each as **Low**, **Average**, or **High** complexity based on its characteristics (e.g., number of fields, number of files referenced).

2. **Calculating Unadjusted Function Points (UFP)**

3. **Applying a Value Adjustment Factor (VAF)** to obtain **Adjusted Function Points (FP)**.

Step 1: Calculate Unadjusted Function Points (UFP)

Each function type has a **weight** depending on its complexity. Using the counts P_i and corresponding weights W_i, the **Unadjusted Function Points** are calculated as per equation 2.1

$$UFP = \sum_{i=1}^{5} \sum_{j=1}^{3} P_{ij} \times W_{ij} \qquad 2.1$$

Table 3: Weight Factors for Function Point Parameters

Parameter / Functional Unit (P)	Weighing Factor (W)		
	Simple	Average	Complex

User Inputs (EI)	3	4	6
User Outputs (EO)	4	5	7
User Enquiries (EQ)	3	4	6
Number of Files (ILF)	7	10	15
External Interface Files (EIF)	5	7	10

Step 2: Value Adjustment Factor (VAF) and Final Function Points

To account for **overall system complexity**, FPA uses **14 General System Characteristics (GSCs)** or complexity factors. Each factor F_i is rated from **0** (no influence) to **5** (strong influence).

Below table shows range of values:

0	1	2	3	4	5
No Influence	Incidental	Moderate	Average	Significant	Essentail

The **Value Adjustment Factor (VAF)** is:

$$VAF = 0.65 + 0.01 \times \sum_{i=1}^{14} F_i \qquad (2.2)$$

The final **Adjusted Function Points (FP)** are then:

$$FP = UFP \times VAF \qquad (2.3)$$

Table 4: 14 General System Characteristics (GSCs)

1.	Data communications – Use of data communication facilities.
2.	Distributed data processing – Presence of distributed processing.
3.	Performance – Required response time or throughput.

4.	Heavily used configuration – Degree of load on the hardware platform.
5.	Transaction rate – Frequency of transactions.
6.	Online data entry – Percentage of data entered online.
7.	End-user efficiency – Design focus on end-user efficiency.
8.	Online update – Number of ILFs updated online.
9.	Complex processing – Extent of logical/mathematical processing.
10.	Reusability – Degree to which the application is designed for reuse.
11.	Installation ease – Difficulty of conversion and installation.
12.	Operational ease – Level of automation for startup, backup, recovery.
13.	Multiple sites – Planned installation at multiple locations.
14.	Facilitate change – Ease with which the system can accommodate future changes.

Benefits of FPA:

FPA is widely used because it:

- **Estimates package size:** Helps determine the size of purchased or existing application packages by counting provided functions.

- **Supports benefit analysis:** Allows users to compare delivered functions with organizational needs.

- **Supports quality and productivity analysis:** Provides a consistent unit ("function point") for measuring **defect density, productivity**, and other performance indicators.

- **Improves resource estimation:** Helps in estimating **effort, cost, and staffing** for both development and maintenance.

Example 2.1: Calculating Function Points

Consider a project where all functions are of **average complexity**, and all 14 GSCs are rated **2 (moderate influence)**. Following is count of each functional units / parameters used:

Parameter	Count	Weight (Average Complexity)	Count X Weight
User Inputs (EI)	40	4	160
User Outputs (EO)	30	5	150
User Enquiries (EQ)	25	4	100
Number of Files (ILF)	6	10	60
External Interface Files (EIF)	4	7	28
	Total UFP		498

Since Each Complexity VAF /GSCs is of moderate category (value 2), VAF as per Equation 2.3 shall be calculated

$$VAF = 0.65 + 0.01 (14 \times 2) = 0.93$$

Finally, the Function Points (FP) are calculated as:

$$FP = UFP \times VAF = 498 \times 0.93 \approx 463$$

Limitations of Function Point Analysis

o **Subjectivity:** The classification and weighting of functions can be subjective and depend on the analyst's expertise.
o **Learning Curve:** It requires understanding and practice to accurately identify and classify functions.
o **Challenges with modern applications:** Rich web applications, microservices, and complex UI/UX patterns can make traditional FPA harder to apply without adaptation.

2.2.1.3 Token count and Halstead's Metrics

Token count measures program size and complexity by treating source code as a sequence of **tokens**, each classified as either an **operator** or an **operand**. This approach underlies **Halstead's software metrics**, which are widely used in tools that analyse code and estimate complexity.

This approach underlies **Halstead's software metrics**, which are widely used in tools that analyse code and estimate complexity.

- **Operators** include: Arithmetic symbols (+, -, *, /), Keywords (while, for, if, return, printf), Special symbols ({}, (), =, ;, ,, []), Function names used as actions (e.g., eof, scanf, sort).

- **Operands** include: Variables, constants, and labels used in the program.

Halstead's idea:

A program is an implementation of an algorithm that can be viewed as a collection of operator and operand tokens.

From these token counts, several base and derived measures are computed.

Halstead's Metrics:

Halstead's metrics are widely used in commercial tools for counting software lines of code and provide several key measures based on token counts. By counting the tokens and determining which are operators and which are operands, the following base measures can be collected:

n_1 = Number of distinct operators.
n_2 = Number of distinct operands.
N_1 = Total number of occurrences of operators.
N_2 = Total number of occurrences of operands.

From these four values, Halstead defines:

1. **Program Vocabulary**

$$n = n_1 + n_2 \qquad (2.4)$$

2. **Program Length**

$$N = N_1 + N_2 \qquad (2.5)$$

3. **Estimated Program Length**

$$\widehat{N} = n_1 \log_2 n_1 + n_2 \log_2 n_2 \qquad (2.6)$$

4. **Program Volume:** Program volume represents the "size" of the implementation in bits, i.e., the space needed to represent the program using the given vocabulary:

$$V = N \times \log_2 n \qquad (2.7)$$

The unit of volume is **bits**.

5. **Program Difficulty:** Difficulty reflects how hard the program is to write or understand:

$$D = \frac{n_1}{2} \times \frac{N_2}{n_2} \qquad (2.8)$$

6. **Program Level:** Program level is the inverse of difficulty; higher level means easier (better) code:

$$L = \frac{1}{D} \qquad (2.9)$$

7. **Programming Effort:** Effort estimates the mental effort needed to implement or understand the program:

$$E = D \times V \qquad (2.10)$$

As a rough guideline:

- Larger **vocabulary** and **volume** $\rightarrow$ more complex program
- Higher **difficulty** and **effort** $\rightarrow$ more error-prone and harder to maintain

Example: Token Count

Table 5: A token Count Example

Operators	Occurrences	Operands	Occurrences
int	4	SORT	1
()	5	x	7
,	4	n	3
[]	7	i	8
if	2	j	7
<	2	save	3
;	11	im1	3
for	2	2	2
=	6	1	3
-	1	0	1
<=	2	-	-
++	2	-	-
return	2	-	-
{}	3	-	-
n1=14	N1=53	n2=10	N2=38

You can now compute:

- Vocabulary $n = n_1 + n_2$

- Length $N = N_1 + N_2$

- Volume $V = N\log_2 n$

- Difficulty $D = \dfrac{n_1}{2} \cdot \dfrac{N_2}{n_2}$

- Effort $E = D \times V$

2.2.2   DESIGN METRICS

Design metrics evaluate structural aspects of the software design that affect **maintainability, testability, and quality**. They help identify parts of the design that are likely to be **error-prone, hard to understand**, or **expensive to change**.

Key design metrics include:

- **Coupling:** Measures the degree of interdependence between modules. Lower coupling is desirable for better modularity and independence. Highly coupled systems are more difficult to maintain, understand, and extend.
- **Cohesion:** Assesses how closely related and focused the responsibilities of a single module are. Higher cohesion within modules is preferred. High cohesion typically results in easier maintenance and improved readability.
- **Complexity Metrics:** Evaluate the complexity of the design, such as Cyclomatic Complexity, which measures the number of linearly independent paths through a program's source code. High complexity can lead to more errors and difficulties in testing and maintaining the software.
- **Lack of Cohesion in Methods (LCOM):** Measures how well the methods of a class are related to each other. Higher values indicate lower cohesion and potential problems in the class design. Classes with low cohesion may require refactoring to improve maintainability and reduce the likelihood of defects.

2.2.3   DATA STRUCTURE METRICS

Data Structure Metrics assess how data is **organized, used, and shared** in a software system. They help identify:

- Data structures that may cause **performance problems**

- Modules that are too tightly **coupled through shared data**

- Areas where maintenance effort may be high because of obscure data usage

Broadly, we can distinguish:

1. **Object-Oriented Data Structure Metrics**

   - Focus on relationships and dependencies in **class hierarchies**.

   - Examples include:

     - **Depth of Inheritance Tree (DIT)**

     - **Number of Children (NOC)**

     - **Weighted Methods per Class (WMC)**

2. **Procedural Data Flow and Usage Metrics**

   - Focus on how data is used in **procedural modules**, including:

     - Amount of data

     - Usage of live variables

     - Program weakness

     - Data sharing among modules

We briefly outline some of these below.

1. Amount of Data

One way to approximate the amount of data in a program is to count the number of items in the **cross-reference list** (variables, constants, labels). In Halstead's terms, this is essentially the number of operands:

$$\eta_2 = \text{VARS} + \text{Constants} + \text{Labels} \qquad (2.11)$$

That is, η_2 equals the **number of operands** in the program.

2. Usage of Data within a Module (Live Variable Metrics)

A variable is **live** at a particular statement if its current value may be used in the future before being overwritten.

- Within a procedure, a variable is live from its **first reference** until its **last reference**.

- The **average number of live variables** in a module gives an indication of how much data is "in play" at any given time.

For a single module, we can compute:
- $L\bar{V}_i$: average number of live variables in the i-th module

For a program with **m** modules, the **average live variable metric** is:

$$L\bar{V}_{program} = \frac{1}{m} \sum_{i=1}^{m} L\bar{V}_i \qquad (2.12)$$

Similarly, we can define **span size**, which counts the number of statements between successive uses of a variable. For a program with **n** modules, the average span size is:

$$S\bar{P}_{program} = \frac{1}{n} \sum_{i=1}^{n} S\bar{P}_i \qquad (2.13)$$

A large span suggests that a variable remains "alive" for many statements, which can make reasoning about the code more difficult.

3. Program Weakness

A program is typically composed of several modules. If modules are **weak** (e.g., low cohesion, many live variables over long spans), the **effort and time** required for development and maintenance increase.

Using:
- $L\bar{V}$: average number of live variables in a module
- γ: average **life** (span) of variables

The **module weakness** can be defined as:

$$W_M = L\bar{V} \times \gamma \qquad (2.14)$$

For a program with **m** modules, the overall **program weakness** can be approximated as:

$$W_P = \frac{1}{m} \sum_{i=1}^{m} W_{M_i} \qquad (2.15)$$

Higher weakness indicates that the program is harder to understand and maintain.

4. Sharing of Data among Modules

Modules often **share data** through global variables, common data structures, or database tables. Excessive data sharing:

- Increases **coupling** between modules
- Makes it harder to **reason about side effects**
- Can lead to subtle **bugs** when one module changes shared data unexpectedly

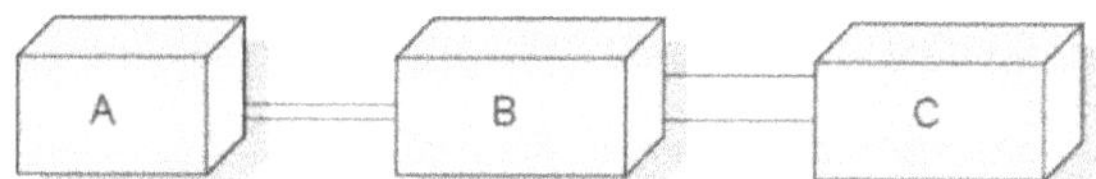

Figure 16:" Pipes" of data shared among the modules

Data-sharing metrics help designers:
- Identify modules that share too much data
- Restructure the system to reduce unnecessary sharing
- Improve **modularity** and **encapsulation**

2.2.4   INFORMATION FLOW METRICS

Information flow metrics are applied to components of a system design to measure the complexity and interdependence among components based on how information flows between them. (Henry & Kafura, 1981). Understanding information flow helps in:

- **Complexity Analysis**: Evaluating the complexity of inter-module communications.
- **Dependency Management**: Identifying and managing dependencies to avoid tight coupling.
- **Testing and Maintenance**: Planning testing strategies based on information flow to prioritize high-risk areas.

2.2.4.1 *Elements of Information Flow Metrics:*

- **Component** - A component is any distinct unit of a software system (e.g., a module, class, or subsystem). Components interact via **function calls**, **data exchange**, or **control signals**.
- **Cohesion** – Cohesion refers to the degree to which the elements within a single component are related and work together to perform a single, well-defined function or task. High cohesion is desirable because it indicates that the component is focused, easier to maintain, and less prone to errors.
- **Coupling** – The degree of **dependency** between components.
    - High coupling → components are strongly linked and harder to change in isolation.
    - Low coupling → components are more independent and the system is easier to manage and extend.

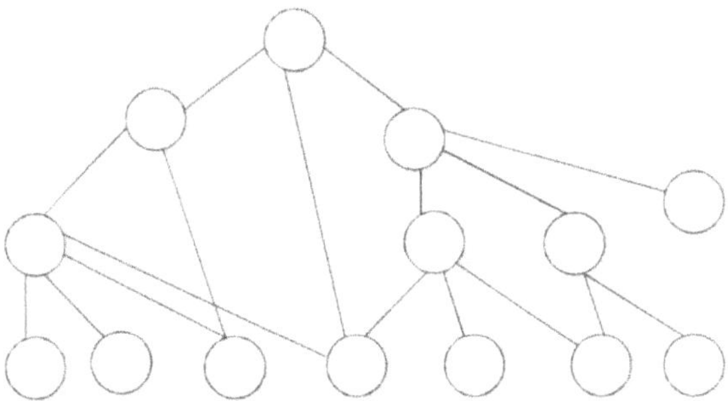

Figure 17: Components of a System Design

BASIC INFORMATION FLOW MODEL

The basic Information Flow Model measures the interaction between modules based on two primary metrics: Fan-in and Fan-out.

Consider a system design fragment, as shown in Figure 17. For a component 'A', the following basic Information Flow Metrics can be defined:

'FAN-IN' – The number of other components that call or pass control to a given component.

'FAN-OUT' – The number of components called by the given component.

Modules with high fan-in are generally stable, as they are relied upon by many others, but they can also become bottlenecks. High fan-out can lead to tight coupling, making changes more difficult.

The **information flow complexity** (or Information Flow Index) of a component A is given by Henry and Kafura as:

$$C_P (A) = [FAN\text{-}IN (A) \times FAN\text{-}OUT (A)]^2 \qquad 2.2$$

Steps to calculate basic Information Flow Metrics

1. **Identify Component(s):** Decompose the system into its constituent components or modules.
2. **Identify the hierarchical level** of each component in the system (top-level components are at the highest level).
3. For Each Component
   a. Calculate number of calls to the component to calculate FAN-IN. Component at Highest level is assigned a FAN-IN of One (instead of Zero)
   b. Calculate number of calls from the component to get FAN-OUT. For Last level of component i.e. which do no call other component, assign FAN-OUT value of one.
   c. Calculate IF Index value of component

4. Sum IF Index Value of each component within each level, which is called as **LEVEL SUM**.
5. **System-wide Aggregation**
   Sum all Level Sums $\rightarrow$ **System Sum** for the entire design.
6. **Ranking and Visualisation**
   - Rank components at each level by **fan-in**, **fan-out**, and **CP(A)**.
   - Plot histograms or line graphs of Level Sums across levels to identify **high-complexity areas** in the architecture.

2.2.4.2 *Extended Information Flow Model:*

The Extended Information Flow Model expands on the basic model by including the number of parameters passed between components and the data elements read or written by a component.

Let,

a= number of components that call A
b= number of parameters passed to A from higher-level components.
c= the number of parameters passed to A from lower-level components.
d= the number of data elements read by A

Then
$$FAN - IN = a + b + c + d \qquad 2.3$$
Also Let.

e= number of components called by A;
f= number of parameters passed from A to higher-level components.
g= number of parameters passed from A to lower-level components.
h = number of data elements written to by A

then,
$$FAN - OUT(A) = e + f + g + h \qquad 2.4$$

These extended metrics give a more detailed picture of how **data and control** flow through the system, beyond simple call counts.

By analysing **fan-in**, **fan-out**, and resulting **information flow complexity**, developers can:

- Identify potential **bottlenecks** and high-risk modules.

- Assess the system's **modularity and coupling**.

- Prioritise components for **redesign, refactoring, or intensive testing**.

Information flow metrics are therefore an important tool for designing **maintainable** and **scalable** software systems.

2.3 EXERCISES

1.1   What do you mean by software metrics? What is the significance of software metrics? Describe any two software size estimation techniques.

1.2   Explain the three main categories of software metrics and provide examples of each.

1.3   Differentiate between Function Point and LOC Software Metrics. Describe the basic steps involved in Function Point Analysis.

1.4   For a program with the number of unique operators $n_1=40$ and number of unique operands $n_2 = 60$, compare
- Program Volume
- Potential Volume
- Program level
- Program Difficulty
- Effort

1.5   Write a short note on the following terms:
- Live variables
- Module Weakness

3   Cost Estimation and Project Planning

After the **Software Requirements Specification (SRS)** is finalized, one of the first management tasks is to estimate:

- Size of the software
- Effort and development time
- Overall project cost

In practice, customers often expect **rough estimates** of cost and schedule even *before* the SRS is fully complete, based on preliminary requirements.

Software project planning includes:

- Effort and cost estimation
- Scheduling and milestone planning
- Resource and staffing decisions

Good planning is critical to deliver a product that:

- Meets **quality** expectations
- Stays within **budget**
- Is completed **on time**

This chapter introduces **cost estimation techniques**, **estimation models**, and **basic project planning concepts**, to underline why careful planning is a non-negotiable part of software engineering.

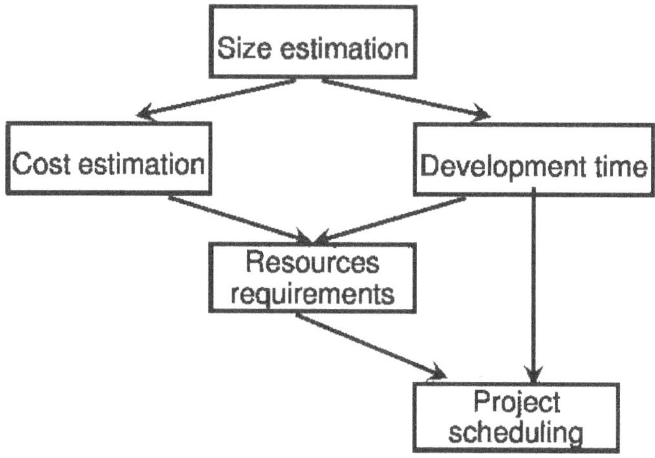

Figure 18: Activities during Software Project Planning

3.1 COST ESTIMATION!

Cost estimation is the process of predicting the **total resources and expenditure** required to complete a software project. It is the basis for:

- Budgeting
- Resource allocation
- Project scheduling and feasibility analysis

Key Characteristics of Cost Estimation

Effective cost estimation usually assumes:

1. **Project scope is reasonably defined**
   Major features, constraints, and interfaces must be understood at least at a high level.

2. **Software metrics are available**
   Size metrics (e.g. LOC, Function Points) and historical data form the basis of quantitative estimates.

3. **The project is decomposed into smaller parts**
Estimation is done on **subsystems or components** and then aggregated, rather than guessing for the whole system in one shot.

3.2 FACTORS AFFECTING COST ESTIMATION

Several factors influence the accuracy and outcome of cost estimates:

1. **Size of the Project**:
   Larger projects typically require more effort, resources, and time, leading to higher costs.

2. **Complexity of the Requirements**:
   Projects with complex functionality, integration, or customization require higher estimation values.

3. **Team Experience and Skills**:
   The experience and proficiency of the team influence the productivity rate and the accuracy of estimates.

4. **Technology and Tools**:
   Advanced tools and technologies may increase initial costs but can reduce long-term maintenance costs.

5. **Environmental and Organizational Factors**:
   Geographically distributed teams, and collaboration tools impact communication and project management efficiency.

3.3 COST ESTIMATION MODELS

Cost estimation models are computational or mathematical frameworks used to predict the costs associated with a project or a product. A model may be static or dynamic.

3.3.1 STATIC MODELS

Static models estimate cost, effort, or other metrics using a fixed set of variables or parameters without accounting for changes over time. Key examples include:

1. **Expert Judgment**: Relies on the expertise of individuals who make estimates based on past experience, without modeling the interactions of different variables over time.
2. **Parametric Estimation**: Uses statistical modeling based on identified parameters, typically not accounting for dynamic interactions among variables.
3. **Bottom-Up Estimation**: Aggregates estimates from lower-level components, usually done at a single point in time.
4. **Top-Down Estimation**
   Estimate the project as a whole and distribute the effort across components.
5. **Basic and Intermediate COCOMO**
   Use static effort equations based mainly on size and a set of cost drivers.
6. **Function Point Analysis (FPA), Feature Points, Use Case Points**
   Use counts of user-visible functionality as the main driver; the relationships are generally static.

3.3.2 DYNAMIC MODELS:

Dynamic models recognize that project variables are **interdependent** and evolve over time. These models simulate how changes in one variable might affect others as the project progresses.

Examples:

- **Detailed/Advanced COCOMO (e.g., COCOMO II with phase-wise breakdown)**

Considers effort distribution across phases and can react to changes in assumptions.

- **PERT (Program Evaluation and Review Technique)** Uses optimistic, pessimistic, and most likely time estimates and updates as more data is gathered.

- **Agile Estimation Techniques** (story points, velocity) Iterative and adaptive; estimates are refined in each iteration based on real progress.

3.4 STATIC SINGLE VARIABLE MODEL

A **static single-variable model** uses one main size parameter, such as **Lines of Code (LOC)** or **Function Points (FP)**, to estimate effort:

$$E = a \times (\text{Size})^b \qquad (3.1)$$

Where:

- E = Effort (typically in **person-months**)

- **Size** = LOC, KLOC, or FP, depending on the model

- a, b = constants derived from **historical data**

These models are simple and easy to apply, but:

- Do not capture variations in **complexity**, **team capability**, or **technology**

- Are less reliable for projects that differ significantly from the historical data used to derive a and b

3.5 STATIC MULTIVARIATE MODEL

A **static multivariate model** uses **multiple factors** to estimate effort or cost, such as:

- Project size
- Complexity
- Team experience
- Tools and environment

These models are more expressive and can account for **interactions** between attributes.

Typical examples:

- **COCOMO family** (size + cost drivers)
- **Walston–Felix model** and other early parametric models

3.6 SPECIFIC ESTIMATION MODELS

3.6.1 SOFTWARE ENGINEERING LAB MODEL (SEL):

The SEL model, introduced by NASA's Software Engineering Laboratory, is a static, single-variable model used for estimating software production. The effort and development time according to the SEL model are calculated as follows: -

Let L= size of software (often in **thousands of lines of code, KLOC**)

Then:

$$E_{SEL} = 1.4 \times L^{0.93} \text{person-months} \qquad (3.2)$$
$$D_{SEL} = 4.6 \times L^{0.26} \text{months} \qquad (3.3)$$

3.6.2 WALSTON-FELIX MODEL

The **Walston–Felix model**, developed at IBM (1977), relates **delivered source code size** L(in **KLOC**) to effort and duration: According to Walston and Felix model, effort is computed by

$$E = 5.2 \times L^{0.91} \text{ Person Months}$$

$$D = 4.1 \times L^{0.36} \text{ Months}$$

Productivity index (I) defined by WALSTON and FELIX uses 29 variables (i= 1 to 29), which are found to be highly correlated to productivity as follows:

$$I = \sum_{i=1}^{29} W_i X_i$$

Where W_i is the weight factor for the ith variable and $X_i = \{-1, 0, +1\}$ the estimator gives X_i one of the values in **-1, 0 or +1** depending on the variable decreases, has no effect or increases the productivity.

Example 3.1: Comparing Walston–Felix and SEL Models

Problem: A software project is expected to require **8 person-years** of effort. Compare the **SEL** and **Walston–Felix** models by estimating the **size of software** (in LOC) that can be produced.

Solution

Manpower involved = 8 Person Years (PY) = 96 (12X8) person-months (PM)

Number of lines of code can be obtained by reversing equation to give

$$L = (E/a)^{1/b}$$

Accordingly,

$$L_{(SEL)} = (96/1.4)^{1/0.93} = 94264 \text{ LOC}$$

$$L_{(Watson\text{-}Felix)} = (96/5.2)^{1/0.91} = 24632 \text{ LOC}.$$

Interpretation:

For the same effort (96 person-months):

- SEL model predicts the team can deliver about 94 KLOC.

- Walston–Felix model predicts about 25 KLOC.

This large difference shows why it is important to:

- Understand the assumptions behind each model

- Use models calibrated with local historical data

- Treat these formulas as guides, not absolute truth

3.7 COCOMO MODEL

The **Constructive Cost Model (COCOMO)** is a widely used empirical model for estimating the **effort, cost, and schedule** of software projects. Developed by **Barry Boehm**, COCOMO uses project **size** (usually in KLOC – thousands of delivered source instructions – or, after suitable conversion, Function Points) and **project type** to predict effort.

COCOMO assumes that projects fall into three **development modes**:

- **Organic (Simple)**
- **Semi-detached (Intermediate)**
- **Embedded (Complex)**

and can be applied at three **model levels**:

- **Basic COCOMO** – quick, rough estimates
- **Intermediate COCOMO** – adds cost drivers (EAF)
- **Detailed COCOMO / COCOMO II** – phase-wise and subsystem-level estimation

3.7.1 COCOMO MODES (PROJECT TYPES)

Each COCOMO **mode** represents a different level of complexity and constraints.

Table 6: COCOMO Modes with Description

Project Mode	Description
Organic (Simple)	Well-understood applications, small teams, stable environment, familiar tools and techniques; limited innovation.
Semi-detached (Intermediate)	Medium-size projects, mixed experience levels, some new aspects or moderate innovation and complexity.
Embedded (Complex)	Software tightly coupled with complex hardware, regulations, and operational procedures (e.g., defence, avionics); high innovation and strict constraints.

3.7.2   BASIC COCOMO MODEL

The **Basic COCOMO** model estimates effort and development time using only **size** (KLOC) and the **mode** of the project.

Effort:
$$E = a \times (\text{KLOC})^b \text{ person-months}$$

Schedule (Development Time):
$$TDEV = c \times (E)^d \text{ months}$$

where:

- E = effort in person-months
- KLOC = thousands of delivered source instructions
- a, b, c, d = mode-dependent constants

For **Basic COCOMO**, the constants are:

Table 7: Basic COCOMO Effort and Schedule Equations

Mode	Effort E(PM)	Schedule $TDEV$(months)
Organic	$E = 2.4 \times (\text{KLOC})^{1.05}$	$TDEV = 2.5 \times (E)^{0.38}$
Semi-detached	$E = 3.0 \times (\text{KLOC})^{1.12}$	$TDEV = 2.5 \times (E)^{0.35}$
Embedded	$E = 3.6 \times (\text{KLOC})^{1.20}$	$TDEV = 2.5 \times (E)^{0.32}$

For **Basic COCOMO**, the **Effort Adjustment Factor (EAF)** is taken as **1** (no extra cost drivers applied). This makes it suitable for

quick "rough order-of-magnitude" estimates early in the project.

Example 3.2 – Basic COCOMO (Embedded Project)

Estimate **effort, schedule, productivity**, and **average staffing** for an **embedded** project with **32 KDSI** (i.e., 32 KLOC), using Basic COCOMO.

For an embedded mode:

$$E = 3.6 \times (32)^{1.20} \approx 230.4 \text{ person-months (PM)}$$
$$TDEV = 2.5 \times (230.4)^{0.32} \approx 14.25 \text{ months}$$

Productivity:

$$\text{Productivity} = \frac{32{,}000 \text{ DSI}}{230.4 \text{ PM}} \approx 139 \text{ DSI/PM}$$

Average staffing:

$$\text{Average staff size} = \frac{E}{TDEV} \approx \frac{230.4}{14.25} \approx 16 \text{ persons}$$

Example 3.3 – Comparing Modes for Same Size, Using 32 KLOC in all three modes:

Table 8: Effort and Schedule for 32 KDSI in Basic COCOMO

Mode	Effort E(PM)	Schedule $TDEV$(months)
Organic	≈ 91.3	$\approx 13.9 \ (\approx 14)$
Semi-detached	≈ 145.5	$\approx 14.3 \ (\approx 14.25)$
Embedded	≈ 230.4	≈ 14.25

Observation: For the same size:

- Effort is **lowest** for **organic**, **highest** for **embedded** (more constraints & complexity).

- Schedule stays in a similar range, but **staffing** (effort per month) must increase for more complex modes.

Intermediate COCOMO Model

The **Intermediate COCOMO** model refines Basic COCOMO by introducing the **Effort Adjustment Factor (EAF)**, which is based on **15 cost drivers**.

Effort: $E = a \times (\text{KLOC})^b \times EAF$ person-months

Schedule: $TDEV = c \times (E)^d$ months

Here:

- EAF = product of 15 cost driver multipliers
- a, b, c, d again depend on the mode (organic, semi-detached, embedded)

Table 9: Intermediate COCOMO Constants

Mode	a	b	c	d
Organic	3.2	1.05	2.5	0.38
Semi-detached	3.0	1.12	2.5	0.35
Embedded	2.8	1.20	2.5	0.32

The **Effort Adjustment Factor** is:

$$EAF = \prod_{i=1}^{15} CD_i$$

where each **cost driver** CD_i is chosen from a rating scale (Very Low, Low, Nominal, High, Very High) and mapped to a numeric multiplier.

Cost Driver Categories (15 Drivers)

1. **Product Attributes**
   - **RELIB** – Required software reliability
   - **DATA** – Database size
   - **CMPLX** – Product complexity
2. **Computer Attributes**
   - **TIME** – Execution time constraints
   - **STORG** – Main storage constraints
   - **VIRT** – Virtual machine volatility
   - **TURN** – turnaround time / response time
3. **Personnel Attributes**
   - **ACAP** – Analyst capability
   - **APEXP** – Application experience
   - **PCAP** – Programmer capability
   - **VEXP** – Virtual machine experience
   - **PLE** – Programming language experience
4. **Project Attributes**
   - **MODP** – Use of modern programming practices
   - **TOOL** – Use of software tools
   - **SCED** – Development schedule (compression/ relaxation)

Table 10: Example Rating Multipliers for Some Cost Drivers (Intermediate COCOMO)

Cost Driver	Very Low	Low	Nominal	High	Very High
RELIB	–	0.75	0.88	1.00	1.15 / 1.40*
DATA	–	–	0.94	1.00	1.08 / 1.16*
CMPLX	0.70	0.85	1.00	1.15	1.30 / 1.65*
TIME	–	–	1.00	1.11	1.30
STORG	–	–	1.00	1.06	1.21
ACAP	1.46	1.19	1.00	0.86	0.71
PCAP	1.42	1.17	1.00	0.86	0.70
MODP	1.24	1.10	1.00	0.91	0.82
TOOL	1.24	1.10	1.00	0.91	0.83
SCED	1.23	1.08	1.00	1.04	1.10

*Exact high/very-high values may vary slightly between sources;

The **Intermediate model** can be applied:

- To the **entire system** early on for rough estimates, or
- To **individual components** in later stages for more accurate estimates.

Example 3.4 – Intermediate COCOMO (Semi-detached Project)

Estimate effort, schedule, productivity, and average staffing for a **semi-detached** system with **58,000 DSI**. Assume:

- Size $\approx$ **58 KDSI** (58 KLOC)

- High main storage constraint $\rightarrow$ **STORG = High = 1.06**

- All other cost drivers at **Nominal** $\rightarrow$ multiplier = 1

So:
$$EAF = 1.06$$

Effort: $\qquad E = 3.0 \times (58)^{1.12} \times 1.06 \approx 300$ person-months

Schedule: $\qquad TDEV = 2.5 \times (300)^{0.35} \approx 19$ months (approx.)

Productivity:
$$\text{Productivity} \approx \frac{58{,}000 \text{ DSI}}{300 \text{ PM}} \approx 193 \text{ DSI/PM}$$

Average staffing:
$$\text{Average staff size} \approx \frac{300}{19} \approx 16 \text{ persons}$$

3.7.3   DETAILED COCOMO AND COCOMO II

Detailed COCOMO extends the Intermediate model by distributing effort across different *phases* and *subsystems*, and by explicitly considering **reuse** and **risk**. Rather than applying one global Effort Adjustment Factor (EAF), it:

- Applies **effort multipliers phase-wise** (requirements, design, coding, testing, integration).

- Allows **different modes and cost drivers** for different subsystems.

- Incorporates **code reuse** and **risk analysis** more explicitly.

Key Characteristics

- **Phase-wise effort multipliers:** Each life cycle phase (planning, design, coding, testing, integration) can have its own cost drivers and multipliers, rather than using a single EAF.

- **Subsystem-level estimation:** Large systems are decomposed into subsystems (e.g., communication, database, GUI).

  - Each subsystem is estimated separately, possibly using different COCOMO modes (organic, semi-detached, embedded).

  - The **total project effort** is obtained by summing subsystem efforts.

- **Phased approach:** Effort is allocated to phases such as:

  - Planning and Requirements
  - System Design (high-level)
  - Detailed Design (modules and interfaces)
  - Module Coding
  - Module/Unit Testing
  - Integration and System Testing

- **Reuse and risk consideration** Detailed COCOMO takes into account:

  - Reuse (adapted code vs new code)

    o   Risk drivers that influence effort and schedule

COCOMO II is the later evolution of COCOMO, designed to handle modern practices such as reuse, incremental development, and object-oriented systems. Conceptually, it follows the same idea—effort is estimated from size plus cost drivers—but with updated parameters and drivers more suited to current technologies.

Example 3.5 – Indian Railways Reservation System

The Indian Railways reservation system is a large **distributed information system** with multiple subsystems (offices across India, central databases, communication networks, and user interfaces). Using Detailed COCOMO (or COCOMO II):

- The **communication subsystem** can be treated as an **embedded** project (tight timing and reliability constraints).

- The **database subsystem** may be estimated as **semi-detached** (moderate complexity, mixed experience).

- The **GUI subsystem** may be treated as **organic** (relatively well understood, user-facing).

Effort for each subsystem is calculated separately using appropriate parameters and cost drivers. The **total effort and schedule** are then obtained by summing across all subsystems and phases.

Practical Application of COCOMO

- COCOMO (especially Intermediate and Detailed/COCOMO II) is most useful for **large-scale projects** with relatively **stable requirements**.

- It is widely applied in domains like **defence**, **aviation**, and **large enterprise systems**, where early, realistic effort and cost estimates are critical.

Limitations of COCOMO-I

- Requires **reasonably detailed project data** (size, drivers) which may not be available in very early stages.

- Delivered Source Instructions (DSI) capture **length**, not conceptual **size**; conversion from higher-level measures (like FP) introduces error.

- Historical calibration data is **difficult to collect and maintain**.

- Original COCOMO was designed for **plan-driven, sequential** life cycles (e.g., waterfall) and does not naturally fit highly **iterative or agile** processes without adaptation.

3.8 PUTNAM RESOURCE ALLOCATION MODEL

The Putnam model is another empirical model that focuses on how staffing (manpower) should be allocated over the project duration. It is based on the observation (Putnam, 1978) that software projects tend to follow a Rayleigh/Norden manpower distribution curve.

The manpower loading Curve is modelled by differential equation

$$m(t) = \frac{dy}{dt} = 2kate^{-at^2} \qquad\qquad \textbf{3.1}$$

= manpower (people/month) at time t

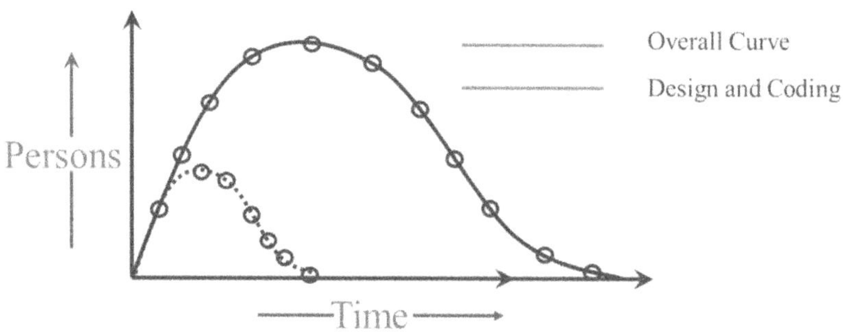

Figure 19: The Rayleigh manpower loading curve

- $y(t)$ = cumulative manpower used up to time t
- K = total effort (area under the curve)
- a, k = model constants

On Integration of equation 3.1 on interval [0, t]

$$y(t) \;=\; K\,[1 - e^{-at^2}] \qquad\qquad \textbf{3.2}$$

Where y(t): cumulative manpower used up-to time t.

$$y(0) = 0; \qquad y(\infty) = k$$

This curve shows how manpower is ramped up during the initial phases, peaks during the most intensive development activities (such as coding and testing), and gradually declines as the project moves toward completion.

- **Initial Phase**: Effort is low due to requirements gathering and initial design activities.
- **Build-Up Phase**: Effort increases rapidly as development and testing intensify.
- **Peak Phase**: The project reaches its maximum staffing level.
- **Decline Phase**: Manpower decreases as testing concludes, defects are fixed, and the product is delivered.

In words, **cumulative effort** starts at zero and grows monotonically towards the total effort K. The Rayleigh curve helps project managers:

- Choose realistic **schedules and staffing levels**.

- Avoid extreme "manpower crashes" at the end or overstaffing at the start.

- Plan resource usage in large, long-duration projects.

The Putnam model has been used heavily in **defence, aerospace,** and **large enterprise** environments, where predictable staffing and schedule planning are essential.

3.9 RISK MANAGEMENT IN SOFTWARE PROJECTS

Risk management is the process of identifying, analysing, prioritising, and controlling potential events that could negatively impact a project's **cost, schedule, or quality**.

Goal of risk management:

Deal with problems while they are still concerns, not crises.

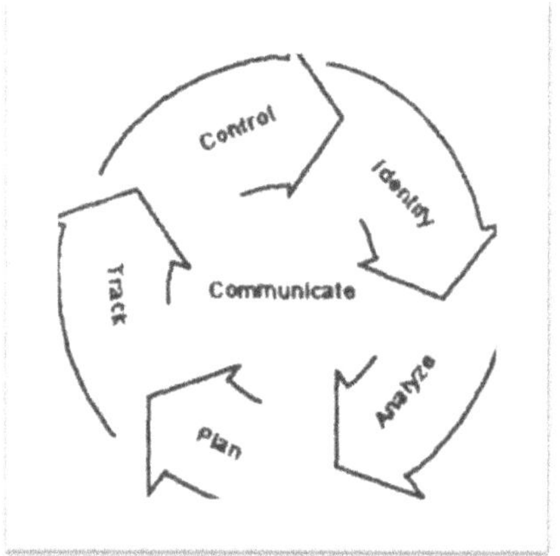

Figure 20: Risk Management Activities

"If you will not actively attack on risks, they will attack on you".

A typical risk management process includes: See Figure 20
1. **Risk Identification** – What can go wrong?
2. **Risk Analysis and Assessment** – How likely and how severe?
3. **Risk Prioritisation** – Which risks matter most?
4. **Risk Planning / Mitigation** – What can we do now to prevent or reduce impact?
5. **Risk Monitoring and Control** – Are risks changing? Are our responses working?
6. **Risk Communication** – Keeping stakeholders informed.

3.9.1   RISK IDENTIFICATION

A software project can be exposed to many different types of risks. **Risk identification** is a systematic attempt to specify threats to the project plan so that:

- Known and predictable risks can be **avoided** where possible, and

- Unavoidable risks can be **controlled** or **mitigated**.

Broadly, we distinguish between:

- **Generic risks:** These are potential threats to almost every software project, for example:

    - Misunderstood requirements
    - Allowing insufficient time for testing
    - Losing key personnel

- **Product-specific risks:** These are unique to the particular project, and can only be identified by people who understand the **technology**, **team**, and **environment** of that project.

The outcome of risk identification is a **list of project-specific risks** that are likely to affect project success and performance.

Typical techniques for risk identification include (Boehm, 1991):

1. **Checklists**

    - A checklist is a list of risks that commonly occur in software projects, compiled from experience on previous projects.

    - It helps ensure that frequently occurring risks (e.g., requirement volatility, interface issues, tool problems) are not overlooked.

2. **Brainstorming**

   - Conducted in group sessions where all team members are encouraged to contribute freely.

   - Participants suggest possible risks; all ideas are recorded without criticism.

   - In subsequent rounds, the list is refined based on discussion, and new risks are added as they emerge.

3. **SWOT Analysis**

   - SWOT stands for **Strengths, Weaknesses, Opportunities, Threats**.

   - The technique examines internal **strengths/weaknesses** and external **opportunities/threats** to identify risks arising from the business, resources, and environment.

4. **Flowchart / Process Method**

   - Models key project activities or processes using diagrams or flowcharts.
   - At each step, ask: What can go wrong here?
   - Helpful for discovering process-related risks and hand-off issues between teams.

These techniques are often used **together** to build a comprehensive risk list, which is then quantified and prioritised in subsequent risk analysis steps.

3.9.2   RISK ANALYSIS

Once risks are identified, the next step is **risk analysis**—turning raw risk data into information that supports decisions.

In risk analysis, we:

- **Classify risks** into categories (technology, schedule, business, etc.).
- **Estimate likelihood and impact** of each risk.
- **Assess overall exposure** so we know where to focus management effort.

Typical **risk categories** in software development include:

- **Technology Risks**

  - Use of new or unproven technologies
  - Lack of or inadequate training on new tools / platforms
  - Poor availability of reliable tools or libraries

- **Performance Risks**

  - Failure to achieve required throughput, response time, or resource usage
  - Inadequate performance benchmarking or stress testing

- **Schedule Risks**

  - Inability to deliver usable software within the committed timeframe
  - Dependencies on external teams or vendors causing delays

- **Quality & Maintainability Risks**

  - Design choices that make the system hard to maintain or extend
  - Poor compatibility with existing systems
  - High probability of defects in critical modules

- **Business Risks**

  - Cost significantly exceeding the planned budget

- o Delivered software not meeting the real business need

- o Loss of market opportunity if the system is delivered too late

The output of risk analysis is usually a **risk list with impact descriptions**, forming the basis for prioritisation and planning.

3.9.3   RISK PRIORITIZATION

Risk prioritisation decides **which risks to address first**. Not all risks are equally dangerous; we must focus on those that can hurt the project the most.

Two key parameters:
- **Probability (P)** – How likely is the risk to occur?
- **Impact (I)** – How serious is the damage if it does occur?

A simple and common tool is a **risk priority matrix** (or risk table), where each risk is rated for probability and impact, for example on scales like Low / Medium / High (or numeric scales like 1–5). Typical steps:

1. For each risk, estimate **Probability** and **Impact**.

2. Compute a simple **priority value** (e.g., Priority = P × I) or classify into categories like:

    - o High probability, high impact
    - o High probability, low impact
    - o Low probability, high impact
    - o Low probability, low impact

3. **Sort the risk list** by descending priority.

In practice:

- **High-probability, high-impact** risks appear at the **top** of the table and must be addressed first.

- **Low-probability, low-impact** risks are placed near the **bottom** and may simply be monitored.

A small sample risk priority table:

Table 8: Sample Risk Prioritization Table

Risk	Category	Probability	Impact
Customer will change requirement	PS	80%	Moderate
Lack of training on tools	DE	80%	Low
Size estimate may be significantly low	PS	60%	Moderate
Delivery deadline will be tightened	BU	50%	Moderate
Funding will be lost	CU	40%	Critical
End-users resist system	BU	40%	Low
Technology will not meet expectations	TE	30%	Critical
Staff inexperienced	ST	30%	Moderate
Larger number of users than planned	PS	30%	Low
...			

3.9.4   RISK PLANNING

After risks are analysed and prioritised, we prepare a **Risk Management Plan**. This plan links each important risk to a **response strategy** and defines what to do if the risk materialises.

A good risk management plan typically specifies, for each major risk:

- **Risk description**
- **Triggers / indicators** (how we will know the risk is about to occur)

- o **Owner** (who is responsible for monitoring and managing it)
- o **Mitigation actions** (what to do in advance to reduce likelihood or impact)
- o **Contingency actions** (what to do if the risk actually happens)

In short:

Deciding in advance how the project will respond to each important risk.

This avoids "panic reactions" later and makes the project more predictable.

3.9.5   RISK TRACKING, MITIGATION AND CONTROL

Once the plan is in place, risks must be **actively monitored** and **controlled** throughout the project.

(a) Risk Tracking and Monitoring

Risk tracking means regularly checking whether:

- New risks have appeared
- Existing risks are increasing or decreasing in severity
- Planned mitigation actions are actually being implemented

Typical monitoring activities include:

- Publishing **project status reports** that explicitly mention key risks and their status.
- Discussing major risks in **regular project meetings** and milestones.
- Watching for **risk triggers** (events or signals indicating that a risk is becoming more likely).
- Updating the **risk register** whenever probability, impact, or ownership changes.

If monitoring shows that a risk is becoming more serious, the project manager may need to:

- Escalate the issue to higher management
- Adjust the **schedule**, **scope**, or **resources**
- Activate contingency plans

(b) Risk Mitigation Strategies

Common high-level strategies include:

- **Accept**
    - Acknowledge that the risk exists and **do nothing special**, beyond monitoring.
    - Used typically for **low-impact** risks where the cost of active management would be higher than the expected loss.

- **Avoid**
    - Change the project so that the risk is removed or its probability becomes negligible.

    - Examples:
        - Modify requirements to eliminate a risky feature.
        - Choose a stable technology instead of a very new, unproven one.
        - Provide incentives and good work conditions to reduce the risk of key staff leaving.

- **Control / Mitigate**
    - Take actions to **reduce the impact or likelihood** of the risk.

    - Examples:
        - Add extra reviews and tests to reduce the risk of defects in critical code.
        - Train team members on a new tool to reduce productivity risks.
        - Add buffer time for risky tasks in the schedule.

When a risk actually materialises, the team should **execute the planned mitigation or contingency actions** rather than improvising under pressure.

3.9.6 COMMUNICATION

Communicate risk status throughout the project is a central and crucial activity during all other risk management activities. Sharing information and getting feedback will substantially increase probability of project success.

3.10 REQUIREMENT ANALYSIS AND MODELLING

A software project may be undertaken to:

- Replace an existing manual system
- Enhance or extend a current computerized system
- Develop an entirely new system to solve a specific problem

Regardless of the type of project, **every system has a purpose**, usually expressed as *what the system should do*. These needs must be clearly understood and agreed upon by both **customers** and **developers** before development begins.

Getting "good" requirements is hard. Defining complete, correct, and consistent requirements is one of the most difficult tasks in software engineering—and also one of the **most expensive to fix** if done incorrectly at a later stage (Brooks Jr, 1995).

Requirements analysis:

- Describes the **operational characteristics** of the software

- Specifies **interfaces** with other system elements (hardware, other software, users)

- Establishes **constraints** (performance, regulatory, hardware limits, etc.) that the software must satisfy

3.11 REQUIREMENTS ENGINEERING

Software requirements engineering is a disciplined, process-oriented approach to the definition, documentation, and maintenance of software requirements throughout the software development life cycle. It ensures that what is built aligns with **stakeholder needs**, is **feasible**, and can be **tested** and **maintained**.

3.11.1 REQUIREMENTS ENGINEERING ACTIVITIES

Some of the common and fundaments steps or activities that are part of requirement engineering are shown in **Figure 21**

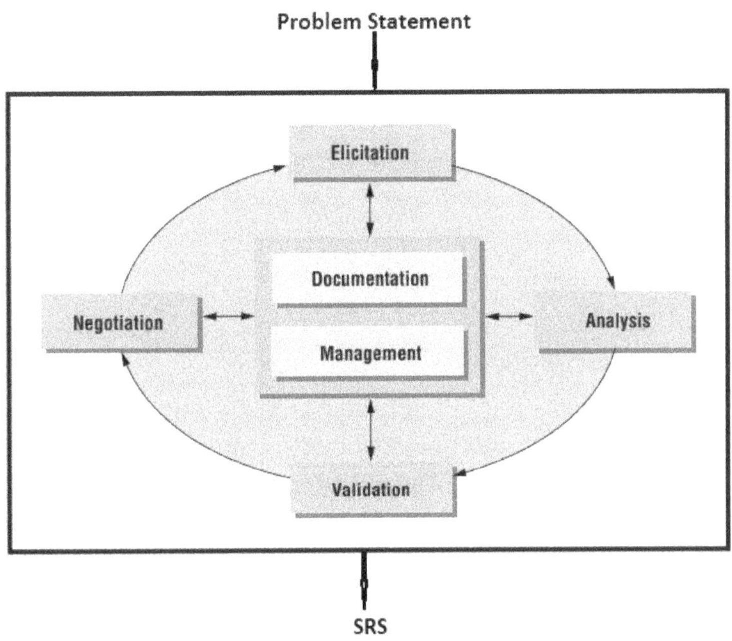

Figure 21: Crucial Activities in Requirements Engineering (Sommerville, 2005)

1. **Inception and Problem Statement**
   Projects begin when a **business need** or **problem** is identified. At inception, we aim for a basic shared understanding of the problem. Typical questions:
   - What is the problem?
   - What is the scope and significance of the problem?
   - What are possible solution options?
2. **Elicitation (Requirements Gathering)**
   - Identify all **sources of information** (stakeholders, documents, existing systems).
   - Discover requirements through interviews, workshops, observation, document analysis, etc.
3. **Analysis**
   - Examine requirements for **overlaps, omissions, inconsistencies, and conflicts**.
   - Classify and organize them (functional vs non-functional, priority, feasibility).
4. **Negotiation**
   - Stakeholders often have conflicting goals and priorities.
   - Resolve conflicts and trade-offs to arrive at a **consistent, agreed set** of requirements.
5. **Documentation**
   - Record the requirements in a clear and structured form that both **stakeholders** and **developers** can understand.
   - The main output is the **Software Requirements Specification (SRS)** document.
6. **Validation**
   - Review the requirements with stakeholders to check:
     - Are these the requirements they *really* need?
     - Are they complete, correct, and testable?
   - This is often done via reviews, prototypes, or walkthroughs.
7. **Management (Requirements Management)**

- o Control inevitable **changes** to requirements.
- o Track versions, status, and impact of each change.
- o Ensure the SRS and related documents stay up to date.

The primary output of requirements engineering is the **SRS**, which often serves as a **contract** between customer and developer.

3.11.2 TYPES OF REQUIREMENTS

Requirements can be viewed from two complementary perspectives.

1. **By customer expectation (Kano-style categories):**

- **Normal Requirements**
    - o Explicitly requested by customers.
    - o If missing, users will be dissatisfied.
    - o Example: "The system must allow users to log in."

- **Expected Requirements**
    - o Often assumed and not always stated explicitly.
    - o Their presence does not delight users, but their absence causes strong dissatisfaction.
    - o Example: Basic performance, reasonable response time, correct outputs.

- **Exciting Requirements**
    - o Not expected by users, but their presence pleasantly surprises them.
    - o Example: Smart recommendations or personalized dashboards.

2. **By behavior (what vs how):**

- **Behavioral Requirements (Functional Requirements)**
    - o Specify **what** the system should do—services, functions, and behaviors.
    - o Example: "The system shall generate a monthly sales report for each region."

- **Non-Behavioral Requirements (Non-functional Requirements)**
    - o Specify **how** the system should perform or behave under certain conditions.
    - o Include reliability, flexibility, maintainability, performance, security, usability, etc.
    - o Example: "The system shall respond within 2 seconds for 95% of queries."

Note: normally we refer, "behavioral" ≈ "functional" and "non-behavioral" ≈ "non-functional".

3.11.3 FEASIBILITY STUDY

A **feasibility study** evaluates whether the proposed project is **worth doing** and **practically achievable**.

Key aspects:
- **Viability of Concept**
    - o Is the basic idea technically and operationally realistic?
- **Cost–Benefit Analysis**
    - o Do expected benefits justify the estimated costs?
- **Business Model**
    - o Is the project financially and strategically sound when current cost and schedule estimates are considered?
- **Product Market**
    - o Is there a clear user base or market for the proposed system?

The result is typically a **feasibility report**, which helps management decide whether to proceed, modify the scope, or cancel the project.

3.12 REQUIREMENT ELICITATION

Requirement elicitation focuses on **discovering** requirements from stakeholders and other sources. Common techniques include:

1. **Interviews**
   - Conduct **open-ended** or **structured** interviews with stakeholders such as end users, managers, and domain experts.
   - Typical questions:
     - What are the problems with the existing system?
     - What do you think are the causes of these problems?
     - What additional functionalities are needed?
     - What are the goals of the proposed system?
2. **Brainstorming Sessions**
   - Group discussions where participants freely suggest ideas, problems, and requirements.
   - Encourages creativity and helps uncover requirements that might not emerge in one-to-one interviews.
3. **Facilitated Application Specification Techniques (FAST)**
   - A **facilitator** organizes a meeting at a neutral site.
   - Participation rules are agreed upon in advance.
   - An agenda is predefined and circulated to participants.
   - The goal is to collaboratively define or refine system requirements.
4. **Quality Function Deployment (QFD)**
   - Translates **customer needs** into **technical requirements**.
   - Requirements are categorized, for example, as:
     - Very important
     - Important
     - Not important but "good to have"

- Not important
- Unrealistic
  - Requirement engineers also judge:
    - Whether a requirement is **easy to achieve**
    - **Complex and should be deferred**
    - **Impossible or impractical** and should be dropped or modified

5. **Use Case Approach**

Use Cases are structured outline or template for the description of user requirements modeled in a structured English like language.

- Use cases explores of how actors interact with the system to achieve a specific goal.
- A **use case** describes a sequence of interactions between an **actor** (person, device, or external system) and the system, leading to a useful outcome.
- A use case is:
  - Initiated by an actor with a goal
  - Considered successful when that goal is achieved

Use cases capture:
  - **Who** (actor)
  - **Does what** (interaction)
  - **With the system**
  - **For what goal**

They focus on *what* the system must do, not *how* it is implemented.

Example – Library Management System Use Cases
  - issue_book
  - check_availability
  - return_book
  - create_user
  - add_new_book

Steps for Use Case Modelling
1. **Identify all users (actors).**
2. **Create a user profile** for each category of user, including all relevant roles they play.

3. **Create a use case** for each user goal and sub-goal.
4. **Structure the use cases**, identifying relationships such as include/extend/generalization (if used in the course).
5. **Review and validate** use cases with users and stakeholders.

3.12.1   USE CASE DIAGRAMS

A **Use Case Diagram** is a UML diagram that graphically represents:

- **Actors, Use cases and Relationships** between them

Basic components are illustrated in Figure 22.

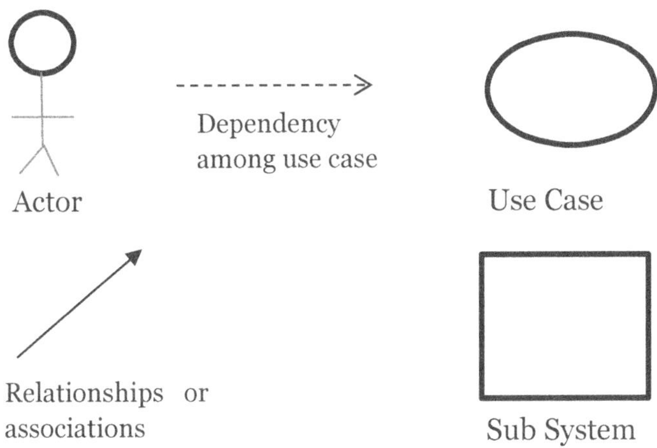

Figure 22: Components of a Use Case Diagram

Key points:
- Use case diagrams represent only the **significant aspects** of the problem domain.
- They describe **what** the system does, not **how** it does it.
- Internal design details are intentionally omitted.

Example 3.6: Use Case Diagram for a Result Management System

Use Cases identified:
a. *Maintain Subject Details*
b. *Maintain Student Lists*
c. *View and Update Marks* – Teachers enter marks for each subject
d. *Generate Result Report* – Admin generates and prints various reports
e. *View Results* – Students view their results
f. *Login* – Used by teachers and admin for authentication to add marks and view reports

Note: Students may only need to **view results**, and may be allowed to do so **without login**, depending on system policies.

Actors identified: Teacher, Admin and Student

A use case diagram connecting these actors and use cases can be drawn as shown conceptually in Figure 23.

Pre- and Post-conditions Example

e.g. for the use case **"View and Update Marks"**:

- **Precondition**:
    - o Teacher must be **logged in** successfully.

- **Postcondition**:
    - o If successful, marks for the selected subject are updated against each concerned student.

    - o If unsuccessful, **no changes** are made to the stored marks.

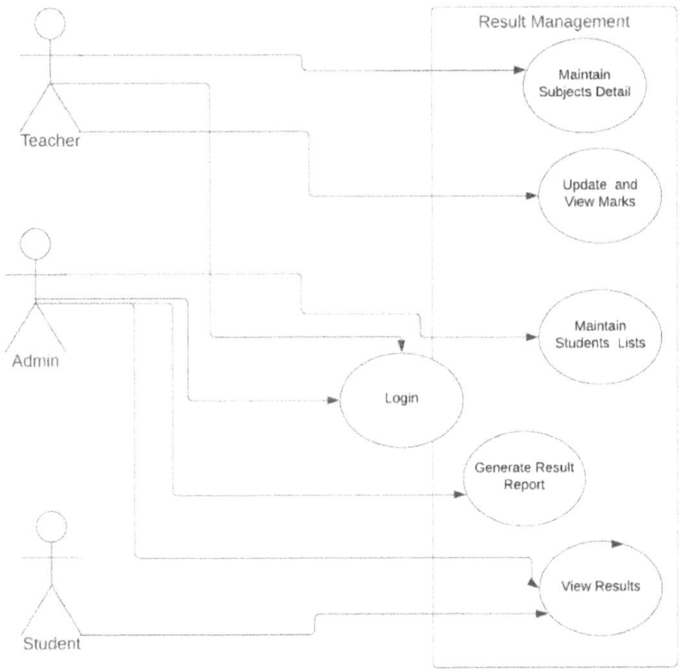

Figure 23: Use Case Diagram for Result Management System

3.13 REQUIREMENT ANALYSIS

After elicitation, the next step is **requirements analysis and modelling**. This often begins with **data modelling** and **process modelling**, for example using:

- Data Flow Diagrams (DFD)
- Entity–Relationship (ER) diagrams
- Class diagrams, etc.

Key Concepts:
- **Data Objects**
  - Represent composite information that must be understood and managed by the system.
  - Have multiple attributes.

- o Examples:
  - ▪ Dimension (with attributes such as width, height, depth)
  - ▪ Customer, Order, Invoice

- **Data Attributes**
  - o Properties of a data object.
  - o Example: For a Car object: body_type, color, engine_capacity.

- **Cardinality and Modality**
  - o **Cardinality**: Number of occurrences of objects of one type related to objects of another type (e.g., one-to-many, many-to-many).
  - o **Modality** (or optionality): Whether the relationship is **mandatory** or **optional** from the perspective of each object.

3.13.1 DATA FLOW DIAGRAMS

Data Flow Diagram (DFD) shows how data moves through a system.

It is a **graphical representation** of:

- **Incoming data flows**
- **Outgoing data flows**
- **Data stores**
- **External entities (sources/sinks)**
- **Processing steps (processes)**

DFDs illustrate the relationships between:
- Data flows
- External entities
- Data stores
- Processing components

Basic DFD components are shown in Figure 24.

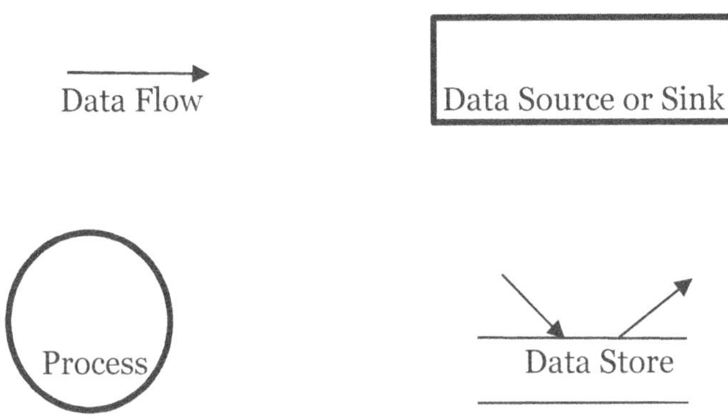

Figure 24: Components of a Data Flow Diagram

To make the DFD more understandable, multi-level DFDs are created. DFDs at higher level are less detailed compared to at lower levels of abstraction. The contextual DFD also call as 0-Level DFD is the highest in the hierarchy.

In the next, Level 1 DFD - processes are further sub-divided into sub processes like 1.1, 1.2 and so on. Similarly, processes are further sub divided in the second level (DFD 2) are numbered like 1.1.1, 2.1.2 and so on. The number of levels depends on the size of the model system.

Zero (0) Level DFD (Context Diagram)

Zero Level DFD also referred as context model Represents the **entire system** as a **single process node**. Incoming and outgoing data from system are represented with arrows. Data Sources/Sinks and Data stores are represented as per DFD notations. As an example, consider a Level 0 DFD for a library management system is shown in Figure 25.

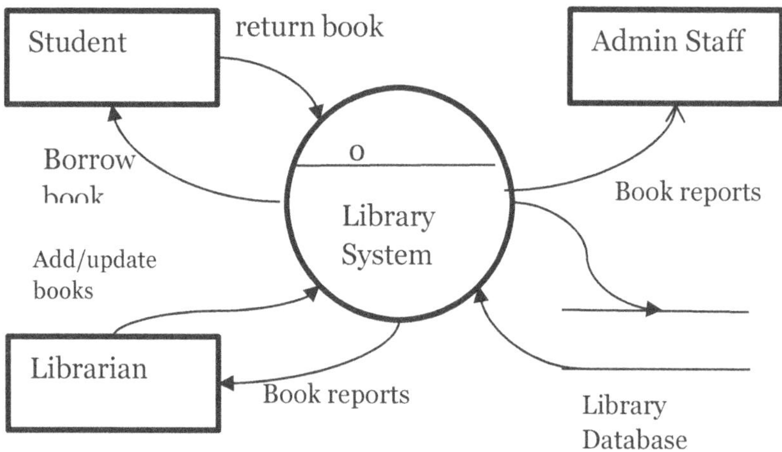

Figure 25: Context Diagram (Level 0 DFD) for Library System

1st Level DFD

In level 1 DFD, the single system node from the level 0 DFD (context diagram) is Decomposed into **major sub-processes**. An Example of level 1 DFD for a Food ordering system is shown in Figure 26.

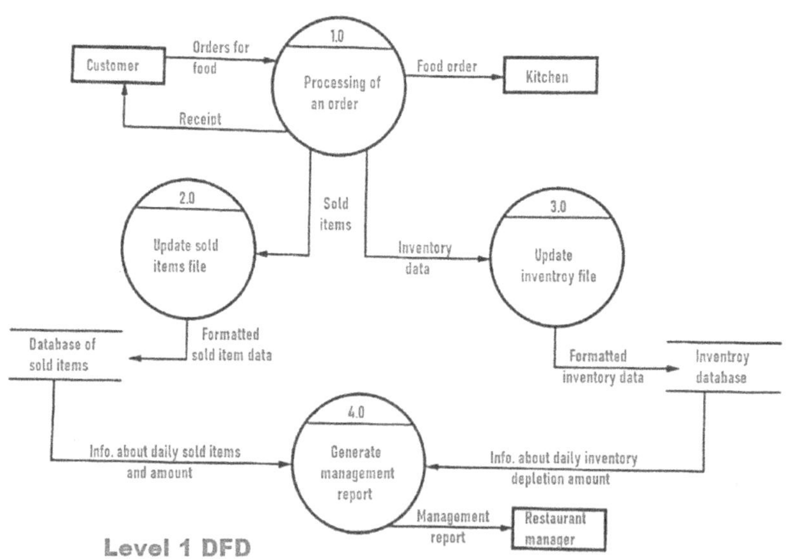

Figure 26: Level 1 DFD for food ordering System

Sub-processes are typically numbered (e.g., 1.0, 2.0, 3.0) and then refined as 1.1, 1.2, etc. Showing, Main processing steps, Corresponding data flows and ata stores used by each process.

Further levels (e.g., **Level 2 DFD**) can be created as necessary, each decomposing a process into more detailed sub-processes. The number of levels depends on the **size and complexity** of the system

3.13.2 DATA DICTIONARIES

A **data dictionary** is a central repository that stores information about all data items used in the system, especially those appearing in **Data Flow Diagrams (DFDs)**.

For each data item, a data dictionary typically records: -

- Name of data Item
- Aliases (other names by which it is known)
- Description and Purpose
- Related data items
- Range of values
- Data Structure Definition (e.g., simple, array, record)

Data Dictionaries are used to -

- Maintain an ordered list of all data items and their subsets
- Search for an item name using its description or vice versa
- Support test-case design, by clarifying input and output data items
- Act as a repository of information about data flows and stores in DFDs

Example 3.7: Data Dictionary for an Online Shopping System

When drawing a DFD for an **online shopping system**, data flow arrows represent the movement of **data items** between:

- Processes (e.g., *Checkout*, *Bank*),
- External entities (e.g., *Customer*), and
- Data stores (e.g., *Order Database*).

For example, in a Level-1 DFD:
- The **Checkout** process may send the following data items to the **Bank** process:
  - OrderID, CustomerID, CartItems, PaymentMethod, PaymentAmount

- This is shown as a **data flow arrow** from *Checkout* to *Bank*.

Data stores (drawn as open-ended rectangles) represent where data is **stored** within the system. They may hold data temporarily or permanently and typically represent tables or files in the underlying database.

Example data dictionary entries for the same system:

Data	Definition	Additional Info
Order ID	Unique identifier for each order.	Data Type: Integer
Customer ID	Unique identifier for each customer.	Data Type: Integer
Product ID	Unique identifier for each product.	Data Type: Integer
Product Name	The name of the product.	Data Type: String, Length: 50
Product Price	The price of the product.	Data Type: Decimal, Range: >0
Cart Items	The list of items in the customer's cart.	Data Type: Array
Payment Method	The method used to process the payment	Data Type: String, Length: 20

Payment Amount	The amount paid by the customer.	Data Type: Decimal, Range: >0

By combining **DFDs** and **data dictionaries**, analysts obtain both:

- A **visual view** of how data moves through the system, and
- A **precise specification** of what each data item means and how it is structured.

3.13.3 ENTITY-RELATIONSHIP (ER) DIAGRAMS

An **Entity–Relationship (ER) diagram** is a detailed **logical representation of data** for an organization. It uses three main constructs:

- **Entities**
- **Relationships**
- **Attributes**

Entity
An entity is any real-world object or concept about which data is stored. Examples (Inventory System): Customer, Vendor, Product, Sale

Relationship
A relationship represents an **association** between two or more entities.
Examples:

- A Customer **is insured by** a Policy
- A Student **enrols in** a Course

Important relationship concepts:
- **Degree of Relationship**: Number of entity types participating in the relationship
  - ○ Unary (1 entity type), Binary (2), Ternary (3), etc.
- **Cardinality of Relationship**: Number of instances of one entity related to instances of another

- o One-to-One (1:1), One-to-Many (1:N), Many-to-Many (M:N)

Basic ER diagram notations (as in Figure 27):
- Entity → rectangle
- Relationship → diamond
- Attribute → oval
- Primary key → underlined attribute

Basic components of an ER diagram are shown in Figure 27

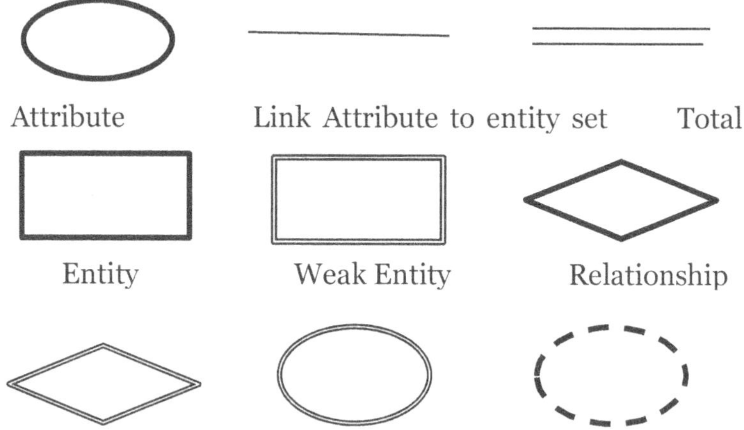

Figure 27: Notations for ER Diagram

3.13.3.1 Weak entity

A weak entity is an entity that **cannot be uniquely identified** by its own attributes alone.

- It **does not have a full primary key** of its own.

- It depends on a **strong (owner) entity** and an **identifying relationship**.

- It has a **partial key** (also called a **discriminator**) that distinguishes its records **only within the context** of the related strong entity.

Examples:

- A Loan entity that cannot exist without a Customer.
- A Dependent entity that cannot exist without an Employee.

Notation for Weak Entities:

- Weak entity set → **double rectangle**
- Identifying relationship → **double diamond**
- Discriminator attribute → **dashed underline**

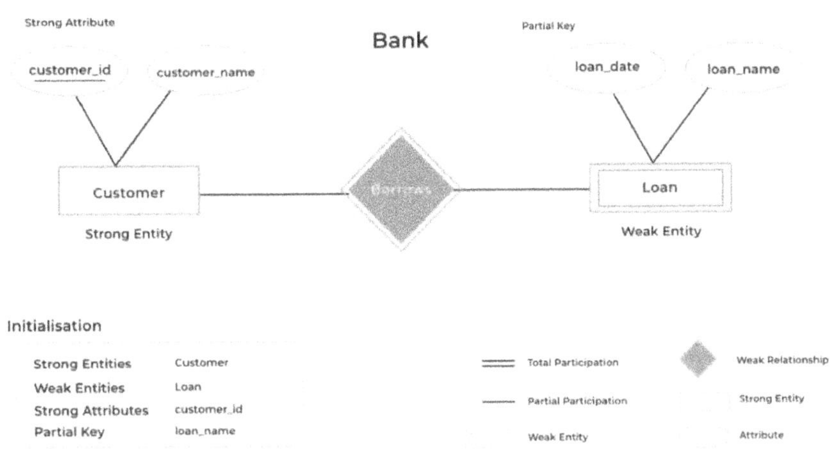

3.14 SOFTWARE REQUIREMENT SPECIFICATIONS (SRS) DOCUMENT

An **SRS** is a document written in natural language that describes **what the system will do**, without specifying **how** it will be implemented.

Importance of an SRS:

- Without a well-written SRS:
    - Developers **do not know exactly what to build**.
    - Customers **do not know exactly what to expect**.
    - Both parties have difficulty deciding **what to validate and test**.

A software requirement may be defined as:

A condition or capability that a system must satisfy to fulfill a contract, standard, specification, or other formally imposed document.

The SRS captures these requirements in a structured, agreed-upon form.

3.14.1 CHARACTERISTICS OF A GOOD SRS

A good SRS should be:

- **Correct**
    - Every requirement stated is one that the system should provide.
- **Complete**
    - All significant requirements are included; no necessary requirement is missing.
- **Consistent**
    - There are **no conflicts** between any set of requirements.
- **Modifiable**
    - The structure and writing make it easy to **update** the document when requirements change.

- **Unambiguous**
    - Each requirement can be interpreted in **only one way**.
    - Avoid vague words such as "fast", "user-friendly", "quickly".

- **Verifiable**
  - There exist **clear methods** (tests, measurements, inspections) to confirm whether a requirement has been met.

  - Example:
    - Not verifiable: "All screens must load quickly."
    - Verifiable: "All screens must load within **5 seconds** under normal load."

- **Traceable**

  - Each requirement can be traced:
    - From its **origin** (stakeholder or business need),
    - To **design elements**, and
    - To the **corresponding code and test cases** (and vice versa).

- **Ranked for Importance and Stability**
  - Requirements should be classified, for example, as:
    - Essential
    - Desirable
    - Optional

  - Each requirement may also be tagged with a **stability indicator** (how likely it is to change).

3.14.2 ORGANIZATION OF SRS

An SRS should follow a clear, logical structure. First two sections are common for all projects, section 3 to 7 is project specific. A typical outline is:

1. **Introduction**
   I. Purpose
   II. Scope
   III. Definitions, abbreviations, and acronyms

IV. Overview of the document
V. References

2. **Overall Description**
(General factors that affect the product)
I. Product Perspective
- o   How the software relates to other system elements and its environment
  II. Product Functions
  III. User Characteristics
- o   Target users, their roles, and educational background
  IV. Constraints
- o   Hardware, software, regulatory, and other constraints
  V. Assumptions and Dependencies

3. **Specific Requirements (System Features)**
I. Functional Requirements
- o   Inputs
- o   Processing
- o   Outputs
- o   Error handling, etc.

4. **External Interface Requirements**
I. User Interfaces
II. Hardware Interfaces
III. Software Interfaces
IV. Communication Interfaces

5. **Non-functional Requirements**
I. Performance requirements
II. Safety and security requirements
III. Quality attributes (reliability, usability, maintainability, etc.)

6. **Other Requirements**
- o   Legal, regulatory, and any domain-specific requirements

7. **Appendices**
   I. Glossary
   II. Analysis models (DFDs, ER diagrams, use case descriptions, etc.)
   III. Preliminary design descriptions, if needed

3.15 EXERCISES

3.1 What are the different activities during software project planning?

3.2 What is feasibility study, explain?

3.3 What are the characteristics of a good SRS?

3.4 Consider the problem of University Result Management System and design the following:
- Use Case Diagram
- Level-1 DFD
- ER Diagram

3.5 What ids DFD? How it is useful? Create Data Flow Diagram and ER-Diagram for Library Management System.

3.6 Draw Zero Level and 1st level DFD for and inventory control system and describe the same briefly.

3.7 Describe use case diagram for an inventory control system. Specify and briefly describe any two important use cases.

3.8 What is requirement engineering? Why it is gaining importance? Discuss different types of requirements and their significance towards quality.

3.9 What do you understand by requirements elicitation. Discuss any two techniques of requirement elicitation in detail.

3.10 Describe facilitated application specification technique (FAST) and compare this with brainstorming sessions.

3.11 What are the risk management activities? Is it possible to prioritize the risks?

3.12 Compare the Walston-Felix model with the SEL model on a software development expected to involve 8 person-years of effort
   I. Calculate the number of lines of source code
   II. Calculate the duration of the development.

3.13 Suppose a project is estimated to be **600 KLOC**. Using the **Basic COCOMO** model, calculate the effort, development time, average staff size, and productivity for each of the three modes:
- Organic, Semidetached, Embedded

4   SOFTWARE DESIGN

Software design is the activity of transforming customer requirements (as specified in the SRS) into a form that can be implemented in a programming language.

A good design is rarely obtained in a single step. Instead, it is refined iteratively through a series of design activities, which are usually divided into two levels:

- **High-Level Design (HLD)**
  Also called *preliminary design*, *architectural design* or *conceptual design*.

- **Low-Level Design (LLD)**
  Also called *detailed design* or *technical design*.

In summary:

- **High-Level Design** focuses on:
  - Identifying major modules and subsystems.
  - Defining control relationships among modules.
  - Specifying interfaces between modules.
  - The outcome is the **software architecture** or **program structure**.
  - A common notation: **structure charts** (tree-like diagrams).

- **Low-Level Design** focuses on:
  - Designing data structures and algorithms within each module.
  - The outcome is a set of **module specifications** (often called module specification documents).

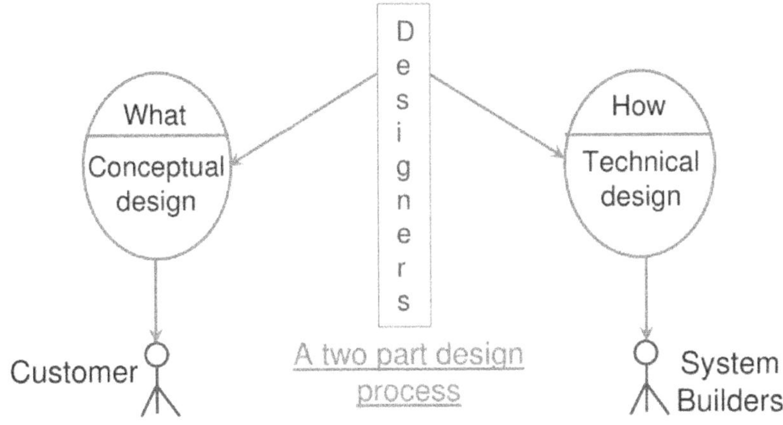

Figure 28: Two Part Design Process

Difference between analysis and design

- **Analysis Phase**
  - Aim: Understand *what* the problem is.
  - Focus: Remove inconsistencies, incompleteness, and ambiguity in the requirements.
  - Output: A clear and validated statement of the problem (SRS).

- **Design Phase**
  - Aim: Provide a model that offers a seamless transition to coding.
  - Focus: Decide *how* the system will meet the requirements.
  - Output: A design model that can be directly implemented.

Conceptual design tries to answer questions such as:
- Where will the data come from?
- What will happen to data in the system?
- How will the system look to users?
- What choices will be offered to users?
- What is the timings of events?
- How will the reports & screens look like?

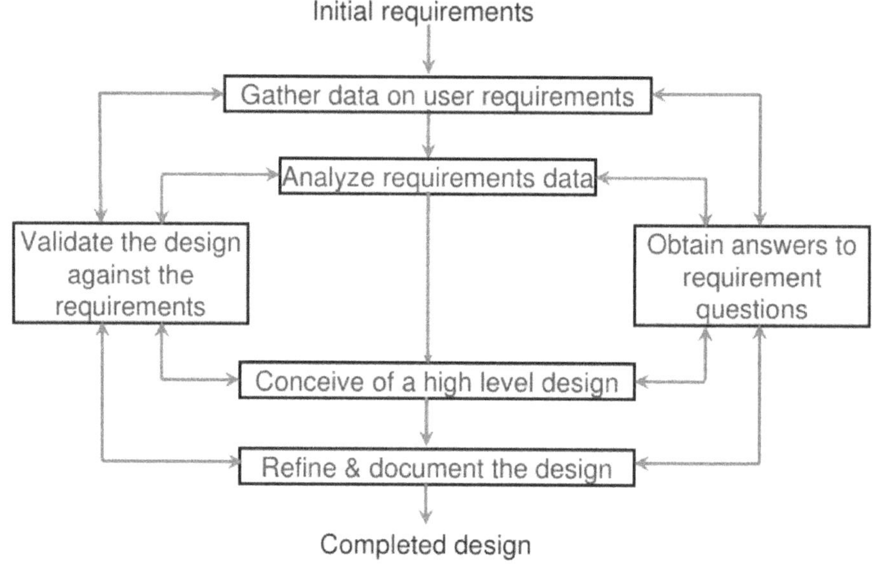

Figure 29: Design Framework

4.1 MODULARITY!

A **modular system** is built from well-defined, manageable units (modules) with clearly defined interfaces among them. Modularity is the property of software that makes a program intellectually manageable.

Benefits of modularity:
- Improves clarity and understandability.
- Simplifies implementation and debugging.
- Facilitates testing and documentation.
- Eases maintenance and future enhancements.

Two key concepts guide modularization decisions:
- **Coupling** – how strongly one module depends on other modules.
- **Cohesion** – how strongly the elements within a module belong together.

Goal: Design modules with **high cohesion** and **low coupling**. Such modules are said to be **functionally independent**.

4.1.1   COUPLING

Coupling between two modules is a measure of how strongly they depend on each other.

- If two modules exchange a large amount of data or control information, they are **highly coupled**.

- Coupling is influenced mainly by **interface complexity**:

  - Number of parameters.
  - Types of parameters.
  - Nature of shared data.

Although coupling is hard to measure precisely, it is useful to classify different types of coupling to qualitatively compare designs.

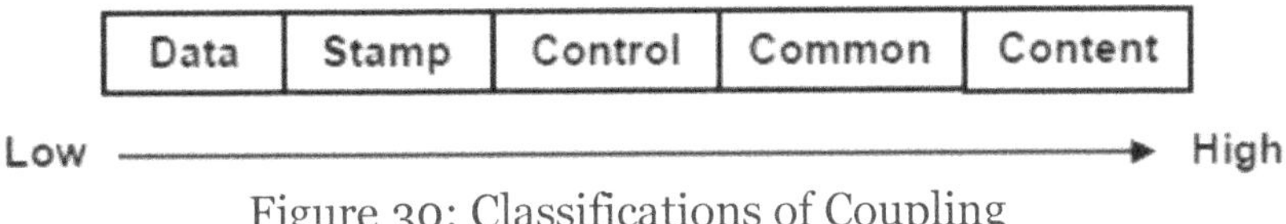

Figure 30: Classifications of Coupling

4.1.1.1   Types of Coupling

Five types of coupling can occur between any two modules. This is shown in Figure 30. From best (lowest) to worst (highest):

- **Data coupling:** Two modules are data coupled, if they communicate through a parameter. An example is an elementary data item passed as a parameter between two modules, e.g., an integer, a float, a character, etc. This data item should be problem related and not used for the control purpose.

- **Stamp coupling:** Two modules communicate by passing a **composite data structure**, such as a `struct` in C or record in Pascal. The called module may not need all fields, which can hide unnecessary dependencies.

- **Control coupling:** exists between two modules, if data from one module is used to direct the order of instructions execution in another. An example of control coupling is a flag set in one module and tested in another module.
- **Common coupling:** Two modules are common coupled, if they share data through some global data items.
- **Content coupling:** Content coupling exists between two modules, if they share code, e.g., a branch from one module into another module.

4.1.2   COHESION

Cohesion is a measure of how strongly the elements within a module are related to each other and work together to perform a single, well-defined task.

- High cohesion: Module is focused, easy to understand, maintain, and reuse.

- Low cohesion: Module does "many unrelated things", harder to test and maintain

4.1.2.1 Types of cohesion

There are seven types/levels of cohesion. The different classes of cohesion that a module may possess are depicted in Figure 31 From best to worst (top to bottom)

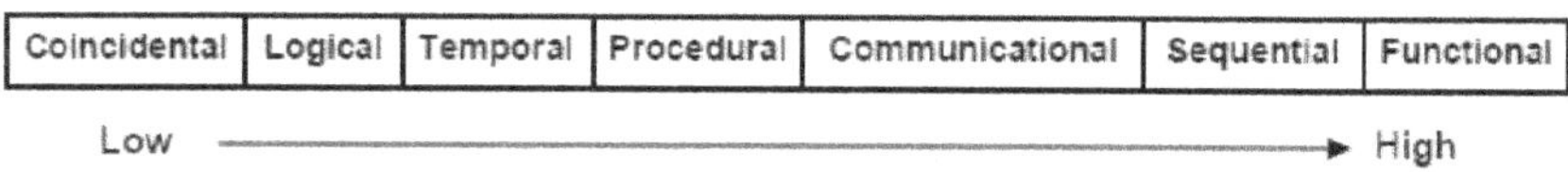

Figure 31: Types of Cohesion

Functional Cohesion: Elements that perform same functional task are put together in a module. It is an ideal situation.

Sequential Cohesion: An element outputs some data that becomes the input for other element, i.e., data flow between the parts.

Communicational Cohesion: Two elements operate on the same input data or contribute towards the same output data. Example- update some record in the database and send to print.

Procedural Cohesion: Elements of procedural cohesion ensure the order of execution. For Example- calculate student awards, print student result, calculate rank, create detailed report.

Temporal Cohesion: A module connected with temporal cohesion all the tasks must be executed in the same time span. For example, classes/modules that initialises, stop or clean something.

Logical Cohesion: The elements are logically related and not functionally. For example, component that perform mathematical operations or do printing task may be grouped together.

Coincidental Cohesion: The elements have **no meaningful relationship** or little conceptual relationship. Any relation among elements of a module is coincidental. It is accidental and the worst form of cohesion.

4.2 CHARACTERISTICS OF A GOOD DESIGN

A good design is critical for project success. It reduces future costs and effort and improves reliability and maintainability.

The characteristics of a good design can be understood by comparing it with a poor design

Table 9

Table 9: Good Design and Bad Design

Attribute	Good Design	Bad Design
Change impact	A change in one part does not usually force changes in many other parts.	A single conceptual change requires changes in many parts of the system.
Logic	Every piece of logic has one and one home.	Logic has to be duplicated.
Nature	Simple, understandable structure	Complex
Cost	Development and maintenance effort is optimal.	Very high
Link	The logic links can easily be found.	The logic links can't be remembered.
Extension	System can be extended with changes in only one place.	System cannot be extended so easily.
Coupling	Low	High
Cohesion	High cohesion within modules.	Low cohesion within modules

4.3 DESIGN STRATEGIES

4.3.1 BOTTOM-UP DESIGN

In **bottom-up design**, the designer starts from **existing low-level components** or utilities and combines them to build higher-level subsystems and, ultimately, the complete system.

- Suitable when:
    - The system is built from **existing modules or libraries**.
    - There is a strong **reuse** of existing components.

Limitation: It may be harder to see the overall system architecture early, because the design emerges from assembling small parts.

4.3.2   TOP-UP DESIGN

In **top-down design**, the designer starts from a **high-level view** of the system and gradually refines it.

Steps:
1. Identify major modules or subsystems.
2. Decompose each module into lower-level submodules.
3. Repeat this refinement until the design is detailed enough to be implemented.

- Suitable when:
    - Requirements and overall system behaviour are **well understood**.
    - The system is being designed **from scratch**.

Issue:
- If coding of top-level modules starts early, **testing** is difficult until lower-level modules are also implemented.
- This can be mitigated by using **stubs** (dummy modules) to simulate lower-level modules during testing.

In practice, many real systems use a **combination** of top-down and bottom-up strategies.

4.3.3   FUNCTION ORIENTED DESIGN

In **function-oriented design**, the system is viewed primarily as a set of **functions** that transform inputs to outputs.

Characteristics:
1. The system is first described in terms of **major functions**.

    o These are then successively refined into **sub-functions**, leading to a hierarchy of functions.

2. The **system state** (i.e., key data structures) tends to be **centralised and shared** among different functions.

Function-oriented design often leads to:
- Hierarchical decomposition of functions.
- Emphasis on **data flow** between functions (often supported by DFDs).
- Use of traditional design notations such as **structure charts, flowcharts**, and **pseudocode**.

4.3.3.1 Design Notations (Function-Oriented)

Design notations are used to represent software design or design decisions. In Function oriented designs, design may be represented with following notations like Structure Charts, Flow Charts and Pseudocode.

Structure Charts: A structure chart represents software architecture design. Main focus in structure chart representation is on the module structure of software and the interaction among different modules. Basic building blocks of a structure chart are shown in Figure 32

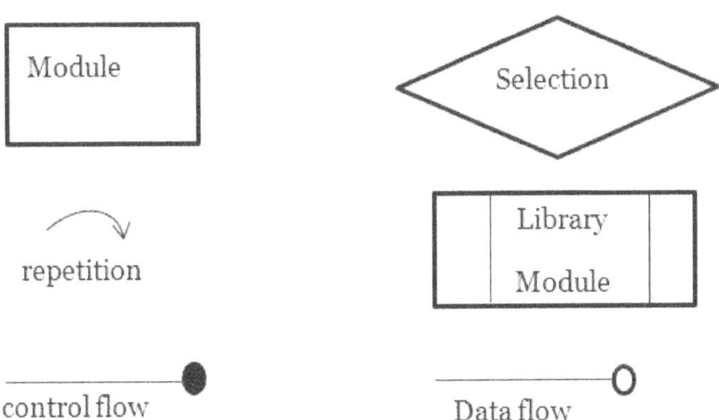

Figure 32: Notations for structure chart

- Rectangles or boxes: represent **modules**.
- Lines/arrows: represent **calling relationships**.
- Annotations on lines: represent **data or control information** passed.

Structure charts are especially useful for illustrating **high-level design (architecture)**.

A structure chart differs from a flow chart as:

A **flowchart** shows the **sequence of control** and decision-making inside a program or a function.

A **structure chart** shows the **hierarchical decomposition** and calling relationships between modules.

- **Flowcharts:**
    - Represent control flow within a program or module.
    - Do **not** represent module boundaries or module hierarchy clearly.
    - Data exchange between modules is not explicitly shown.

- **Structure Charts:**
    - Represent **module hierarchy** and call relationships.
    - Show **data interchange** between modules via parameters.
    - Do **not** show internal control flow within modules.

In summary:
- Use **flowcharts** to describe *how a single module works internally*.
- Use **structure charts** to describe *how modules are organised and interact*.

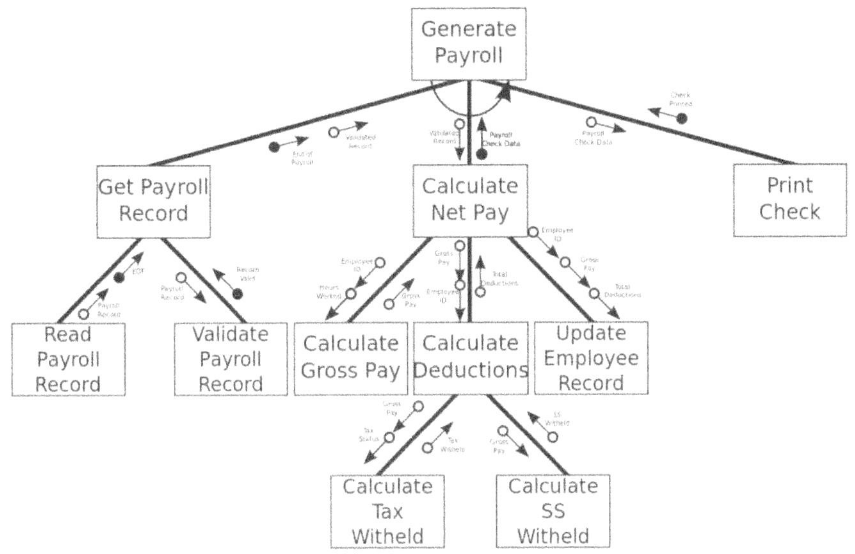

Figure 33: Structure chart for payroll management

Pseudocode

Pseudocode is an informal, structured description of the logic of a program or module using:
- Natural-language phrases, and
- Programming-like control constructs such as IF–THEN–ELSE, WHILE, FOR, REPEAT–UNTIL, LOOP, BEGIN–END, etc.

Advantages:
- Easy to read and write.
- Independent of any specific programming language.
- Serves as a bridge between **design** and **code**.

Pseudocode is often used for:
- Specifying **algorithms** during the design phase.
- Supporting **code walkthroughs** and **peer reviews**.
- Ensuring that the logic is complete before coding begins.

4.3.4   OBJECT ORIENTED DESIGN

In **object-oriented design (OOD)**, the system is viewed as a collection of **objects** that model real-world entities. Instead of focusing on functions such as sort() or display(), OOD focuses on entities such as **Employee**, **Product**, **Account**, etc.

An **object** is characterized by:

- **State** – information stored in attributes (data).
- **Behavior** – operations or methods that act on this state.

Unlike function-oriented designs where state is often kept in centralized shared data structures, in OOD the state is **distributed** among objects. Objects communicate with one another by **message passing** (method calls).

To model object-oriented systems, we typically use **UML (Unified Modeling Language)** diagrams. UML provides a standard graphical language to represent and document software systems.

Common UML diagram types include:

- Use Case Diagrams
- Class Diagrams
- Sequence Diagrams
- State and Statechart Diagrams
- Activity Diagrams
- Object Diagrams
- Interaction Diagrams (including communication diagrams)
- Component and Deployment Diagrams

Typical steps in designing an object-oriented system:

- Identify and design appropriate UML diagrams based on the application requirements.

- Prepare and review a **Design Document** capturing the static and dynamic structure of the system.

4.3.4.1 *Use-Case Diagram*

A use case diagram is used to represent what happens when an actor interacts with the software system. It demonstrates significant functional aspects of the system (not going in implementation details or design issues). Use case diagrams are discussed in detail in Section 3.12.

4.3.4.2 *Activity Diagrams*

Activity diagrams are used to show the **flow of control** from one activity to another. An **activity** represents an operation or step that changes the state of the system. They are useful for:

- Describing workflows
- Modeling business processes
- Showing parallel and conditional flows in a process

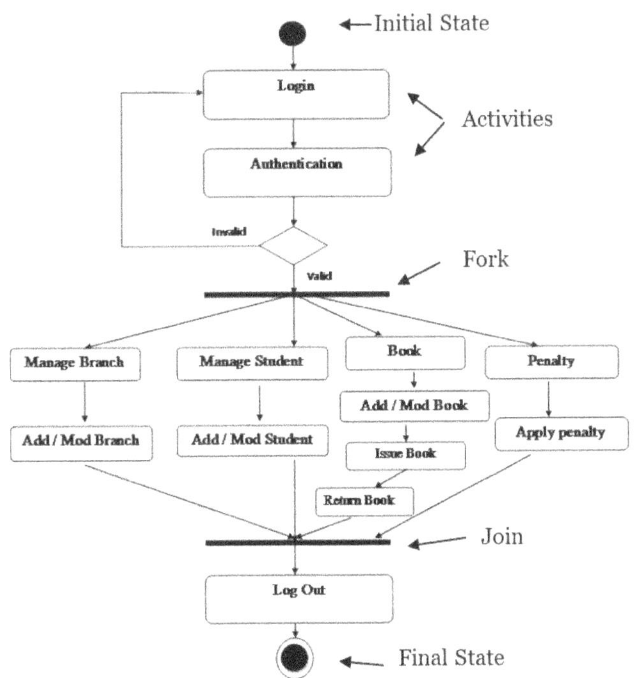

Figure 34: Activity Diagram for Library Management System

Used to show from of control from one activity to the other. Here an activity represents an operation on some objects in a system that results in a change in the state of a system.

4.3.4.3 Interaction Diagram

Interaction diagrams help visualize the **dynamic behavior** of a system by modeling how objects interact through message passing.

Their purposes include:

- Capturing the dynamic (run-time) behavior of a system
- Describing the flow of messages between objects
- Showing how objects collaborate to realize a use case

Interaction diagrams are commonly of two main types:

1. **Communication (Collaboration) Diagrams**

   - Represent the **structural organization of objects** and the messages exchanged between them.
   - Show objects as vertices and messages as labeled links (arcs).
   - Emphasize relationships among objects.

2. **Sequence Diagrams**

   - Show objects arranged along the horizontal axis and **time flowing from top to bottom**.

   - For each **use case**, we can create a sequence diagram that details:

     - Which objects participate
     - What responsibilities each object has
     - In what order messages are sent

This helps in assigning responsibilities to classes and objects during design.

One of the major goals of design is to determine the classes and their responsibilities and one way of represent that is **creating a sequence diagram** for each **use case** we identify in the analysis stage. We break down the system into a number of objects and decide what each object should accomplish in the corresponding use case. That is, we delegate responsibilities. We move from top to bottom to show a sequence of events.

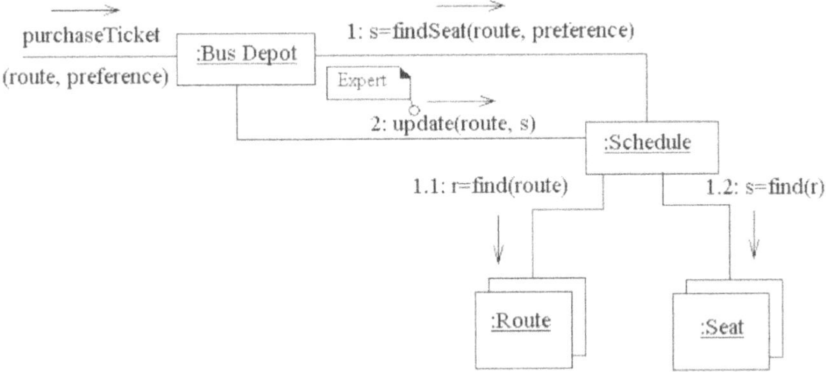

Figure 35: Example of a Collaboration Diagram (Bus Ticket Issue)

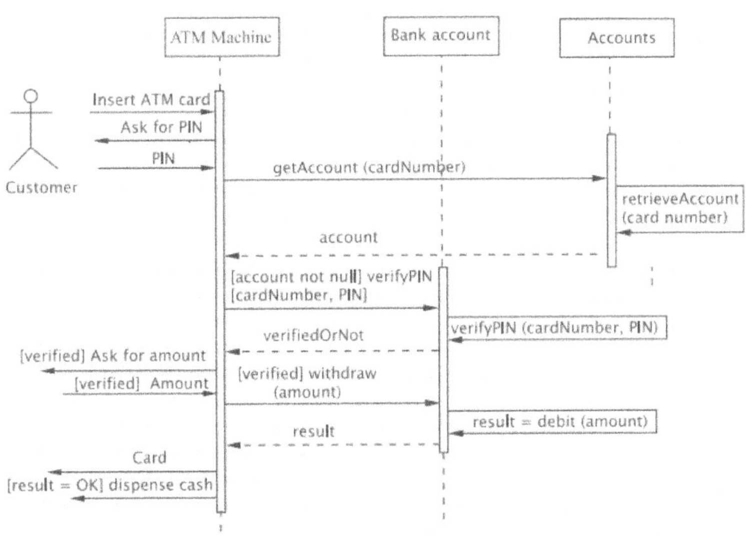

Figure 36: Sequence Diagram Example

4.3.4.4 Class Diagram

A **class diagram** is the primary UML diagram for representing the **static structure** of an object-oriented system. It shows:
- Classes and their attributes and operations
- Relationships between classes

Common relationships include:
- **Association** – A general connection between two classes (e.g., *Customer places Order*).
- **Dependency** – One class depends on another (e.g., uses it as a parameter or local variable).
- **Aggregation** – A "whole–part" relationship where the part can exist independently (e.g., *Team–Player*).
- **Generalization (Inheritance)** – A specialization relationship (e.g., *Employee* is a general class, *Teacher* and *Clerk* are subclasses).

Various Notation used are shown below. [1]

Association
Dependencies
Aggregations

Generalizations.

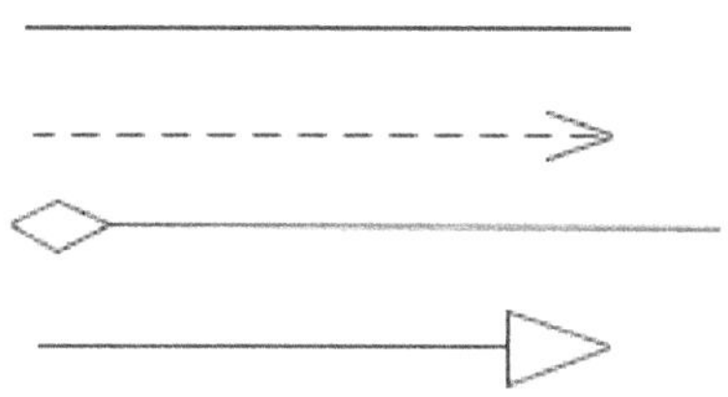

4.3.4.5 State Chart and Object Diagrams

A **state diagram** is used to represent the condition of the system or part of the system at finite instances of time. An **object diagram** represents a snapshot of the system at a particular moment, showing object instances and their links, corresponding to a a class diagram at run time.

---

[1] A Class is a set of objects that share a common structure and behavior. e.g., objects of class 'student' may represent a group of different students that belongs to class 'student'. In other words, classes act as blueprint of objects.

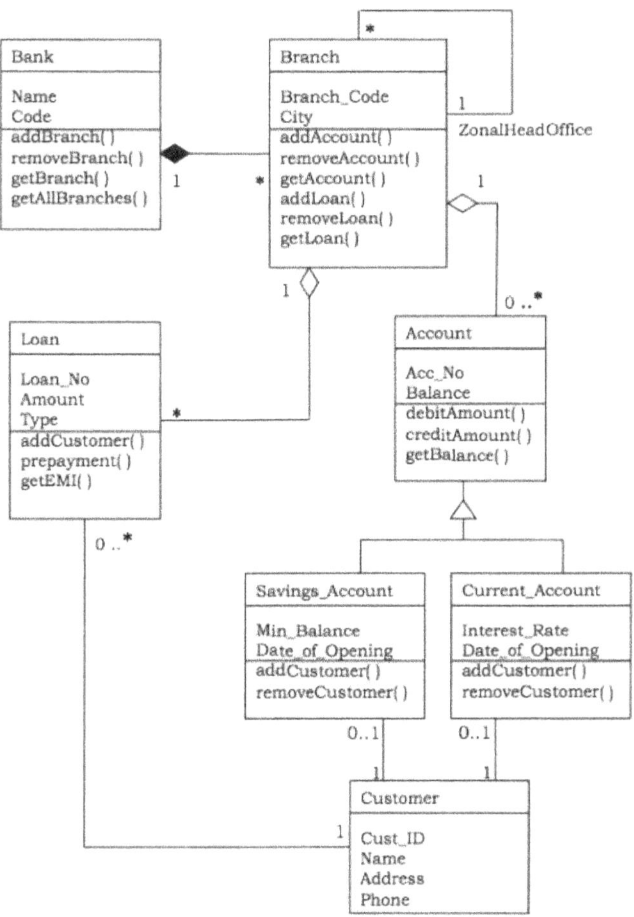

Figure 37: A class diagram Example

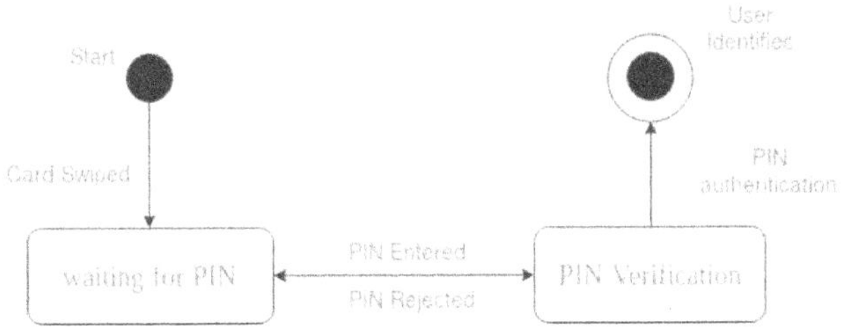

Figure 38: Example of a State Diagram

4.3.4.6 Component and Deployment Diagrams

Component diagrams represent the structural view of a system, showing how the software components (or modules) interact and depend on each other.

These diagrams are particularly useful during the implementation phase to map out the physical pieces of code that compose the software.

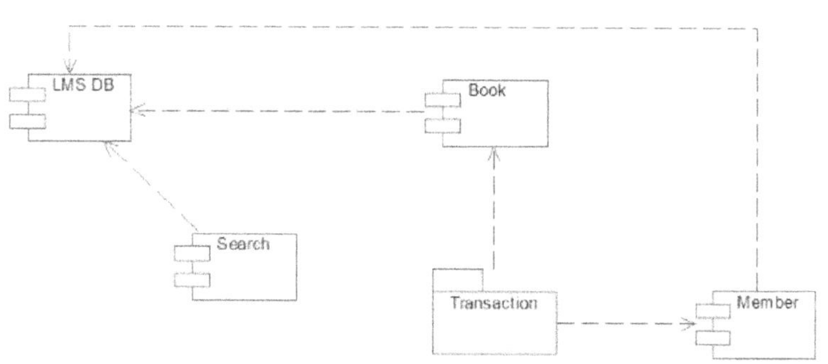

Figure 39: Example of Component Diagrams

Deployment Diagram Deployment diagrams show the physical deployment of artifacts (software applications, libraries, or services) on hardware nodes (servers, devices, etc.).

They describe:

- **Nodes** (e.g., application server, database server, client machine)
- **Artifacts** (e.g., .war files, executables, libraries)
- The mapping of artifacts onto nodes

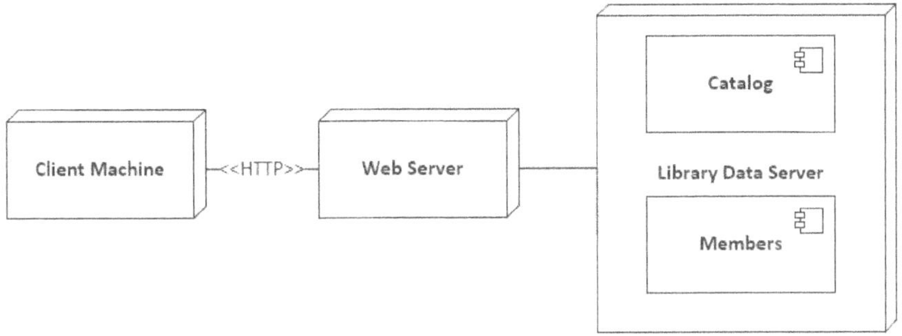

Figure 40: Deployment Diagram Example

4.3.4.7 Detailed Design Document

The Detailed Design Document (DDD) presents the architecture of the system and the static and dynamic architecture of its main components. The **Detailed Design Document** describes:

- The overall **architecture** of the system
- The **static structure** (classes, interfaces, components, data structures)
- The **dynamic behavior** (interactions, state changes, workflows) of the main components

It usually includes:
- Class and object-level designs
- Detailed descriptions of methods, parameters, and algorithms
- Database schema and data design
- Interface specifications (APIs, web services, external interfaces)

The DDD ensures that developers have all necessary information to:
- Implement the modules
- Write unit and integration tests
- Deploy the system consistently

The document ensures that developers have all the necessary information to write code, test, and deploy the system successfully.

4.3.4.8 User Interface Design!

User Interface (UI) Design focuses on creating intuitive, efficient, and visually appealing interfaces that enhance user interaction with a software system. It bridges the gap between users and the underlying system functionality, ensuring accessibility and usability.

Key Elements of UI Design:

1. **Navigation:** Menus, tabs, and breadcrumbs to help users move through the application.

2. **Forms and Inputs:** Input fields, dropdowns, checkboxes, and buttons.

3. **Typography and Icons:** Choose readable fonts and appropriate font sizes.

4. **Colours and Themes:** Use colour schemes that align with the brand and ensure readability.

5. **Responsive Design:** Ensure the interface works seamlessly across devices (desktop, tablet, mobile).

6. **Feedback Mechanisms:** Status indicators, progress bars, tooltips, alerts, and error messages to inform the user about system status and actions.

4.4 PROGRAMMING STYLE

Programming style refers to the style of writing the source code for a computer program to avoid errors and keep is easier to debug and maintain.

Good programming style supports the larger goals of software engineering: clarity, correctness, and maintainability.

4.4.1   ELEMENTS OF PROGRAMMING STYLE

The goal of good programming style is to provide understandable, straightforward, elegant code. The programming style may be derived from the coding standards set for a programming language, as well as the preferences of the programmer.

Most organizations define their own **coding standards**, which developers are expected to follow. Typical elements include:

- **Use of Global Variables:** Global variables should be minimized or avoided to reduce unintended interactions and enhance modularity. If used, they should be named distinctly to avoid conflicts.
- **Standard Header Information to put in modules** like Module Name, Date of creation, Author, modification history and its description etc.
- **Naming conventions for variables:** Clear, consistent naming for variables, functions, classes, and files (e.g., camelCase, snake_case, PascalCase).
- **Error and Exception handling:** Use consistent mechanisms to handle errors and exceptions, avoiding silent failures.
- **Ease of understanding:** Avoid overly complex expressions. Prefer clear logic and structure.
- **Single Purpose Identifiers:** Not to use an identifier for multiple purposes even for temporary entities.
- **Comments and Documentation:** Code should be well documented with proper comments
- **Function/Method Size:** A function should not be very lengthy
- **Control Structures:** Avoid unconditional loops as they makes program difficult to understand.

A consistent programming style helps teams read and understand each other's code and simplifies long-term maintenance.

4.4.2   CODE REVIEWS

Code reviews are systematic examinations of source code by one or more developers other than the original author. They are carried out after a module compiles and runs successfully (i.e., is free from syntax errors).

Goals of code reviews:

- Detect logic and design defects early
- Improve code quality and consistency
- Promote knowledge sharing within the team

Two common forms of code review are **walkthroughs** and **inspections**.

Code Walkthroughs

A few members of development team are given task of read and understand the code, followed by simulation of code execution by hand (dry runs) results of these executions are documented and put in subsequent meeting to discuss.

Objectives:

- Check logical correctness and adherence to design.
- Detect algorithmic and logical errors.
- Identify opportunities to simplify and optimize the code.

Code Inspections

- Focus on discovering typical coding errors due to oversight or incorrect practices.

- Do **not** usually involve executing or simulating code; instead, they rely on careful reading.

Common issues checked:

- Use of **uninitialized variables**
- **Array index** out-of-bounds risks

- Incorrect use of **logical operators** or misunderstanding of operator precedence
- Inconsistent types, style, or formatting

A strong programming style combined with regular code reviews is fundamental to producing **reliable, maintainable, and scalable** software.

4.5 EXERCISES

4.1 What is Software Design? What are principles of software design? Illustrate.

4.2 Differentiate between Good Design and bad Design.

4.3 Define module cohesion and list down various types of cohesion. Which of the following is the worst type of module cohesion?

4.4 Which is the best type of coupling and which one is worst type of coupling? Explain with examples.

4.5 What is meant by programming style? What are important elements of programming style? Discuss

5   SOFTWARE RELIABILITY

Software systems are developed to assist humans in performing tasks more efficiently and accurately. To achieve this, once software is deployed, it must be reliable, providing users with confidence in its accuracy, security, and data integrity. Reliability is a key attribute in both hardware and software.

Consider a case where a user has prepared a critical presentation for a board meeting. If, at the last moment, a software failure (due to a bug) prevents access to this file, the result may be a serious setback—lost business, reputational damage, or both. Situations like this highlight the importance of software reliability.

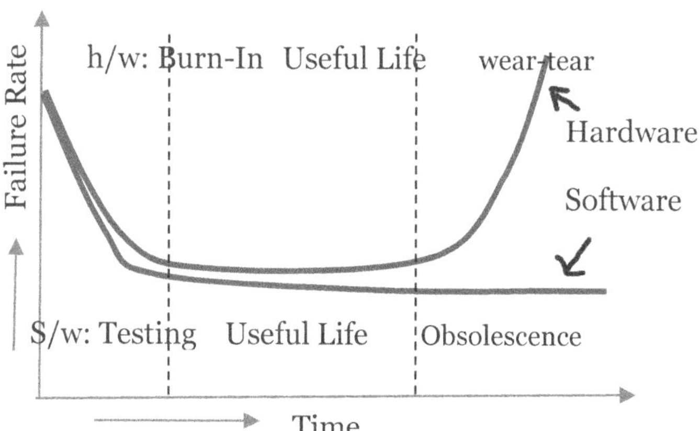

Figure 41: Reliability Curve for Hardware and Software

Hardware vs Software Reliability

For hardware, reliability generally follows a three-stage lifecycle: burn-in, useful life, and wear-out. Initially, "burn-in" failures may occur, after which the hardware enters a stable "useful life" period with a low failure rate. Eventually, the "wear-out" phase is reached, where the failure rate increases due to aging. This cycle, when plotted as failure rate over time, forms a **"bathtub" curve** as shown in Figure 41.

For software, however, reliability is not affected by physical wear and tear. Instead, software faces obsolescence due to evolving technological environments, infrastructure changes, or new user requirements.

Consequently, a reliability curve for software would show spikes in failure rates during major updates or operational complexities but lacks the "wear-out" phase seen in hardware.

Figure 42: Software failure

Definition of Software Reliability

According to the IEEE Standard Glossary:

"Software reliability is the ability of a system or component to perform its required functions under stated conditions for a specified period of time."

Another common definition is:

"Software reliability is the probability of failure-free operation of a computer program for a specified time in a specified environment."

So, reliability is inherently **probabilistic** and **time/condition dependent**.

Key Terms: Error, Bug, Fault and Failure

These terms are often mixed up, but they have distinct meanings in software engineering:

- ➢ **Fault (Defect in code/design)**
  - o A *static* defect introduced during development.
  - o Example: Wrong formula coded, missing input validation, incomplete implementation.
  - o A fault may exist for a long time before it is actually executed.
- ➢ **Error (Incorrect internal state)**
  - o Occurs when a fault is executed, leading to an incorrect internal state.
  - o Example: Division by zero caused by missing range checks; array index going out of bounds.
- ➢ **Bug (Informal term)**
  - o General, informal term for a fault/defect that causes incorrect or unexpected behavior.
  - o Discovered during testing or in production.
- ➢ **Failure (Externally visible incorrect behaviour)**
  - o The system does not perform a required function or does not meet performance/behavioural requirements.
  - o Example: Payment gateway fails to process valid transactions during peak hours.

Relationship Between the Terms:

- A **fault** is introduced in design or code.
- When executed, it produces an **error** (incorrect state).
- This error may manifest as a visible **failure**.
- The fault causing this may be informally referred to as a **bug**.

Failure Time and Frequency

To analyse and model software reliability, we must measure failures carefully. Important quantities include:

- **Time of failure** – Exact timestamp when each failure occurs.

- **Time between failures** – Interval between consecutive failures, indicating stability.

- **Cumulative failures over time** – Total number of failures experienced up to a given time.

- **Failure frequency in an interval** – Number of failures in a specific time window.

Such data is the input for reliability growth models and helps decide when the software is "good enough" for release.

Objectives of Software Reliability Engineering

Software reliability engineering aims to:

- Quantify software reliability in **measurable terms**.

- Identify, remove, or reduce faults throughout the lifecycle.

- Apply engineering principles to design and implement failure-resistant software.

- Use mathematical **models** to predict failure behaviour and guide testing and release decisions.

5.1 SOFTWARE RELIABILITY MODELS

Reliability models help quantify the reliability of software systems and predict how reliability improves as testing progresses.

Software Reliability Growth Models mathematically describe how reliability improves as we:

- Execute the software,
- Observe failures, and
- Correct the underlying faults.

They help answer questions such as:

- How many more failures are expected if we continue testing?

- How long do we need to test to reach a target failure intensity?

- When can we realistically stop testing and release the product?

A reliability growth model typically expresses **reliability** or **failure intensity** as a function of Time, or the number of failures detected/removed.

5.1.1   MUSA'S BASIC EXECUTION TIME MODEL

Basic execution time model (developed by J.D. Musa) is among the foundational reliability growth models and is based on execution time. (Musa & Okumoto, 1983)

Reasons for popularity:

- Practical and conceptually simple.
- Parameters relate clearly to real-world quantities.
- Useful for relatively accurate reliability prediction.

The model is based on **execution time** (CPU time actually spent running the software), which can later be converted to calendar time.

Failure Intensity as a Function of Mean Failures

Let:

- $\lambda(\mu)$= current failure intensity (failures per unit CPU time)
- λ_0= initial failure intensity
- μ= mean (expected) number of failures experienced so far
- V_0= total expected number of failures over the life of the software (as time $\rightarrow \infty$)

Musa's model uses:

$$\lambda(\mu) = \lambda_0 \left(1 - \frac{\mu}{V_0}\right) \qquad\qquad \textbf{5.1}$$

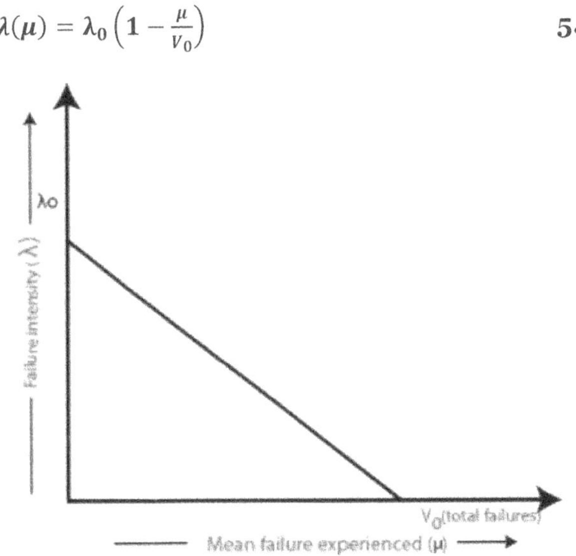

Figure 43: Failure Intensity (λ) versus mean failure (µ)

As more failures are detected (µ increases), the failure intensity decreases linearly until it approaches zero when nearly all faults have been removed.

The rate of change of failure intensity with respect to µ is:

$$\frac{d\lambda}{d\mu} = -\frac{\lambda_0}{V_0} \qquad (5.2)$$

(i.e., it decreases at a constant rate as failures are discovered and fixed.) Figure 43.

5.1.2 MEAN FAILURES AS A FUNCTION OF EXECUTION TIME

Let τ be execution time (e.g., CPU hours).

From reliability theory and Musa's assumptions, the relationship between mean failures and execution time can be written as:

$$\frac{d\mu}{d\tau} = \lambda_0\left(1 - \frac{\mu}{V_0}\right) \qquad (5.3)$$

Solving this differential equation gives:

$$\mu(\tau) = V_0\left(1 - e^{-\frac{\lambda_0 \tau}{V_0}}\right) \qquad (5.4)$$

So:

- Initially ($\tau = 0$), $\mu(\tau) = 0$.
- As $\tau \to \infty$, $\mu(\tau) \to V_0$ (we approach the total number of latent faults).

Failure Intensity as a Function of Execution Time

From (5.1) and (5.4), we can express failure intensity directly in terms of execution time:

$$\lambda(\tau) = \lambda_0 \, e^{-\frac{\lambda_0 \tau}{V_0}} \qquad (5.5)$$

This is an exponential decay: as more CPU time is used in testing, failure intensity decreases. *Figures 43–45 illustrate these relationships between μ, λ and τ.*

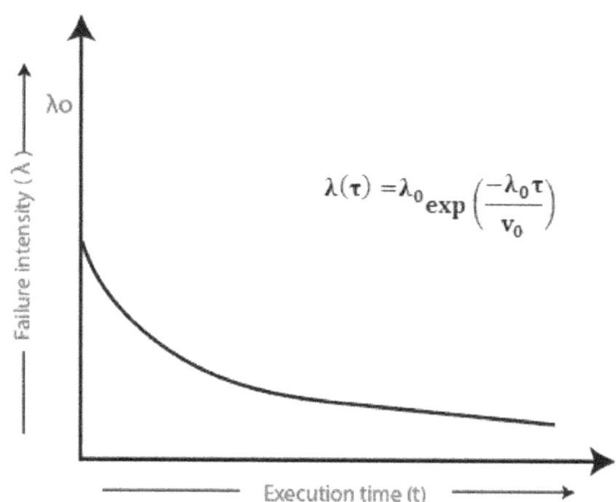

Figure 44: Failure Intensity with respect to Execution Time

5.1.3 ADDITIONAL METRICS FROM MUSA'S MODEL

Given a **current failure intensity** λ_1 and a **target failure intensity** λ_2, we can compute:

- **Additional expected failures** $\Delta\mu$ to reach the target:

$$\Delta(\mu) = \frac{V_0}{\lambda_0}(\lambda_1 - \lambda_2)$$

- **Additional execution time** $\Delta\tau$ required to reach that objective.

$$\Delta(\tau) = \frac{V_0}{\lambda_0} \ln\left(\frac{\lambda_1}{\lambda_2}\right)$$

Example 5.1: A program is expected to experience $V_0 = 100$ failures in infinite time. It has currently experienced $\mu = 40$ failures. The initial failure intensity was $\lambda_0 = 10$ failures/CPU hour.

1. Calculate the current failure intensity.
2. Calculate the number of failures experienced after 10 and 50 CPU hr of execution.
3. Calculate the failure intensities at 10 and 50 CPU hr of execution.
4. Calculate the expected number of failures that will be experienced and the execution time between a current failure intensity of 3 failures/CPU hr and and objective of 1 failure/CPU hr.

Solution:

Here, $V_0 = 100$, $\mu = 40$ and $\lambda_0 = 10$ failure/CPU hr

1. Current Failure Intensity at 40 failures
$$\lambda(\mu) = \lambda_0\left(1 - \frac{\mu}{V_0}\right)$$
$$= 10\,(1 - 40/100) = 6 \text{ failures/CPU hr}$$

2. Failure experienced after 10 CPU hr

$$\mu(\tau) = V_0\left(1 - e^{\left(\frac{-\lambda_0 \tau}{V_0}\right)}\right)$$

$$= 100(1 - e^{-1}) = 100\ (1 - 0.367) \approx 63 \text{ failure}$$

Failure experienced after 50 CPU hr (At $\tau = 50$)

$$\mu(50) = 100\left(1 - e^{\left(-\frac{-10\ x\ 50}{100}\right)}\right)$$

$$= 100\ (1 - e^{-5}) \approx 99 \text{ failure}$$

3. Failure intensity at 10 CPU Hr

$$\lambda(\mathbf{10}) = 10\ e^{\left(-\frac{10*10}{100}\right)}$$

$$= 10\ *\ e^{-1} = 3.67 \text{ failure/CPU Hr}$$

Failure intensity after 50 CPU hr

$$\lambda(\mathbf{50}) = 10\ e^{\left(-\frac{10*50}{100}\right)}$$

$$= 10\ *\ e^{-5} = 0.067 \text{ failure/CPU Hr}$$

4. **Additional failures and execution time** to go from current $\lambda_1 = 3$ failures/CPU hr to target $\lambda_2 = 1$ failure/CPU hr.

$$\Delta(\mu) = \frac{\mathbf{100}}{\mathbf{10}}(3 - 1) = \mathbf{10}\ (2) = 20 \text{ failure}$$

$$\Delta(\tau) = \frac{\mathbf{100}}{\mathbf{10}}\ ln\left(\frac{3}{1}\right) = 10 * 1.0986 \approx 11\ CPU\ Hr$$

5.1.4   MUSA-OKUMOTO LOGARITHMIC POISSON MODEL

Logarithmic Poisson execution time model, also known as **Musa-Okumoto model**, assumes that all faults are equally likely to occur and are independent of each other. This model is particularly useful when failure data exhibit a logarithmic reduction in failure intensity over time.

The failure intensity as a function of cumulative failures (μ) is:

$$\lambda(\mu) = \lambda_0 \, e^{-\theta\mu}$$

Here, θ is decay parameter for failure intensity and λo is initial failure intensity

Rate of Change of Failure Intensity w.r.t. μ is given by

$$\frac{d\lambda}{d\mu} = -\lambda_0 \theta \, e^{-\theta\mu} = -\theta\lambda$$

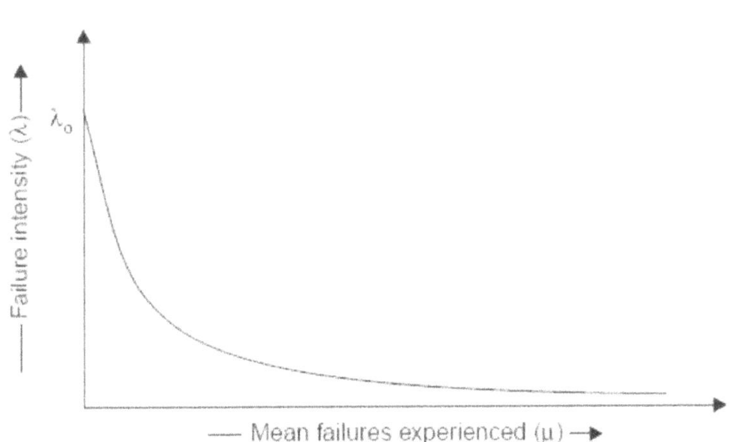

Figure 45: Logarithmic Poisson Model: Relationship between failure intensity (λ) and mean failures (μ)

This model is particularly suitable when empirical data shows a logarithmic decline in failure intensity. It may predict higher initial failure intensity than the basic model in cases of long execution times or rapid initial failure discovery.

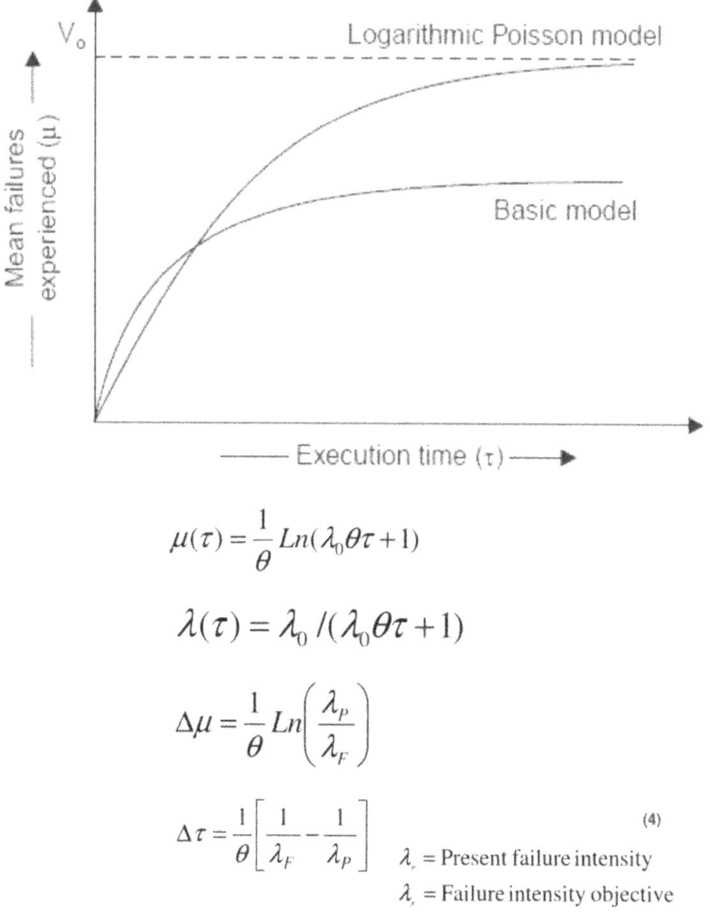

$$\mu(\tau) = \frac{1}{\theta} Ln(\lambda_0 \theta \tau + 1)$$

$$\lambda(\tau) = \lambda_0 / (\lambda_0 \theta \tau + 1)$$

$$\Delta\mu = \frac{1}{\theta} Ln\left(\frac{\lambda_P}{\lambda_F}\right)$$

$$\Delta\tau = \frac{1}{\theta}\left[\frac{1}{\lambda_F} - \frac{1}{\lambda_P}\right] \qquad (4)$$

λ_r = Present failure intensity

λ_r = Failure intensity objective

Example 5.2: Assume that the initial failure intensity is 20 failures/CPU hr. The failure intensity decay parameter is 0.02/failures. We have experienced 100 failures up to this time. Using Logarithmic Poisson execution time model find

(i) Determine the current failure intensity.
(ii) Calculate the decrement of failure intensity per failure.
(iii) Find the failures experienced and failure intensity after 20 and 100 CPU hrs. of execution.
(iv)Compute the additional failures and additional execution time required to reach the failure intensity objective of 2 failures/CPU hr.

$$\lambda_0 = 20 \text{ failures/CPU hr.}$$
$$\mu = 100 \text{ failures}$$
$$\theta = 0.02 \text{ / failures}$$

(i) Current failure intensity:

$$\lambda(\mu) = \lambda_0 \exp(-\theta\mu)$$

$$= 20 \exp(-0.02 \times 100)$$

$$= 2.7 \text{ failures/CPU hr.}$$

(ii) Decrement of failure intensity per failure can be calculated as:

$$\frac{d\lambda}{d\mu} = -\theta\lambda$$

$$= -.02 \times 2.7 = -.054/\text{CPU hr.}$$

(iii) (a) Failures experienced & failure intensity after 20 CPU hr:

$$\mu(\tau) = \frac{1}{\theta} Ln(\lambda_0\theta\tau + 1)$$

$$= \frac{1}{0.02} Ln(20 \times 0.02 \times 20 + 1) = 109 \; failures$$

$$\lambda(\tau) = \lambda_0 / (\lambda_0\theta\tau + 1)$$

$$= (20)/(20 \times .02 \times 20 + 1) = 2.22 \; failures / CPU \; hr.$$

(b) Failures experienced & failure intensity after 100 CPU hr:

$$\mu(\tau) = \frac{1}{\theta} Ln(\lambda_0\theta\tau + 1)$$

$$= \frac{1}{0.02} Ln(20 \times 0.02 \times 100 + 1) = 186 \; failures$$

$$\lambda(\tau) = \lambda_0 / (\lambda_0\theta\tau + 1)$$

$$= (20)/(20 \times .02 \times 100 + 1) = 0.4878 \; failures / CPU \; hr.$$

(iv) Additional failures $(\Delta\mu)$ required to reach the failure intensity objective of 2 failures/CPU hr.

$$\Delta\mu = \frac{1}{\theta} Ln \frac{\lambda_P}{\lambda_F} = \frac{1}{0.02} Ln\left(\frac{2.7}{2}\right) = 15 \text{ failures}$$

$$\Delta\tau = \frac{1}{\theta}\left[\frac{1}{\lambda_F} - \frac{1}{\lambda_P}\right] = \frac{1}{0.02}\left[\frac{1}{2} - \frac{1}{2.7}\right] = 6.5 \text{ CPU hr.}$$

5.1.5 CALENDAR TIME COMPONENT OF THE BASIC EXECUTION MODEL

So far, we have discussed reliability in terms of **execution time** τ(e.g., CPU hours). In practice, we care about **calendar time** t(days/weeks of testing) and the **resources** used.

The **calendar time component** adds resource constraints to the basic execution time model. Let:

- θ_r = amount of resource r required per unit of execution time (e.g., tester-hours per CPU hour).
- μ_r = resource r required per failure (e.g., debugging hours per failure).
- $\mu(\tau)$ = mean failures experienced after execution time τ.

Then, the **expected total resource usage** x_r up to execution time τ is:

$$x_r = \theta_r \tau + \mu_r\, \mu(\tau) \qquad\qquad \textbf{5.2}$$

The change in resource usage per unit of execution time is calculated by differentiating with respect to execution time:

$$\frac{dx_r}{d\tau} = \theta_r + \mu_r \frac{d\mu}{d\tau} = \theta_r + \mu_r \lambda(\tau)$$

Now suppose:

- P_r = available quantity of resource r (e.g., testers).
- ρ_r = utilization of that resource (fraction of time actually used).

Then the **effective available resource per unit calendar time** is $P_r\rho_r$. By equating the resource consumption rate to the available rate, we relate **calendar time** and **execution time** as:

$$\frac{dt}{d\tau} = \frac{\theta_r + \mu_r\lambda(\tau)}{P_r\rho_r}$$

This equation allows us to convert from the reliability growth expressed in execution time back into **calendar time**, accounting for constraints such as limited test staff or machine time.

Example 5.3 – *A team runs test cases for 12 CPU hours and identifies 30 failures. Each hour of execution requires 4 person-hours of test effort. Each failure requires 1 person-hour, on average, to verify and classify. Compute the total failure identification effort required.*

Given:
- $\tau = 12$ CPU hours
- $\mu(\tau) = 30$ failures
- $\theta_r = 4$ person-hours per CPU hour
- $\mu_r = 1$ person-hour per failure

Using (5.6):

$$x_r = \theta_r\tau + \mu_r\mu(\tau) = 4 \times 12 + 1 \times 30 = 48 + 30 = 78 \text{ person-hours}$$

So, **78 person-hours** of effort are required for this portion of testing and failure identification.

5.2 RELIABILITY ALLOCATION

Reliability allocation is the process of **distributing a system-level reliability goal** across its individual components or modules so that:

- The **overall system reliability target** is met, and
- The **total cost** (testing, debugging, and design effort) is minimized.

This concept is important for both **hardware** and **software** systems.

In software, especially for systems composed of *sequentially executed* modules (where at most one module runs at a time):

- Each module can be tested and debugged independently.
- Each module is assigned its **own reliability objective** (e.g., a target failure rate).
- If every module meets its target, the **combined system** meets the overall reliability goal.

Methodology for Reliability Allocation

A typical reliability allocation procedure involves:

1. **Define Allocation Objective:**
   Decide whether you are:
   - Fixing a **system-level failure rate / reliability target**, or
   - Working under a **fixed testing budget** (time, staff, cost).

2. **Set Constraints**

   - Maximum allowed failure rates per module, or
   - Maximum allowable testing effort/cost per module.

3. **Obtain Reliability-Growth Parameters:**
   For each component, estimate or identify reliability-growth model parameters (from testing history or prior similar projects).

4. **Analyse Component Interactions**
   Determine whether components are:

   - Independent, or
   - Interacting (e.g., shared resources, interfaces). For interacting components, obtain pair-wise or joint failure rate data if needed.

5. **Solve the Allocation Problem**

   - If a **closed-form analytical solution** exists, derive component-level reliability targets directly.

   - Otherwise, use **numerical or mathematical programming techniques** (e.g., optimisation methods) to minimise total cost subject to system reliability constraints.

6. **Use Reliability Allocation Tools (Optional)**
   In practice, reliability allocation and optimisation are often supported by tools such as **BlockSim** or similar reliability modelling software.

Example 5.4: Consider a simple system with **three components** in series. Assuming independent component reliabilities R_1, R_2, R_3, the **system reliability** is:

$$R_S = R_1 \cdot R_2 \cdot R_3$$

Suppose, target overall system reliability is 95%, then using above equation we get:

$$0.95 = R_1 \cdot R_2 \cdot R_3$$

Our task is to solve for R1, R2 and R3 satisfying above equation to obtain an optimum solution, we also need to use our cost functions (i.e., define the total allocation costs including cost involved in testing, failure identification and correction) as:

$$C_T = C_1(R_1) + C_2(R_2) + C_3(R_3)$$

Where, $C_i(R_i)$ is the (increasing) cost of testing, fault removal, and design improvements needed to achieve reliability R_i for component i.

The **optimal allocation problem** is:

- Find values of R_1, R_2, R_3 such that:

    - The constraint $R_1 R_2 R_3 \geq 0.95$ is satisfied, and
    - The total cost C_T is **minimised**.

In practice, this is solved using reliability allocation and optimisation techniques (analytical or tool-based), yielding reliability targets for each component that collectively meet the system reliability goal at **minimum total cost**.

5.3 EXERCISES

5.1   What is Software Failure? How it is related to Fault?

5.2   What is software reliability? Compare hardware reliability with software reliability.

5.3   Define the following terms in software reliability:
- Failure intensity
- Mean time between failures (MTBF)
- Fault, error, and failure
- Reliability growth

5.4   Suppose the initial failure intensity is 50 failure/CPU hours, failure intensity decay parameter is 0.01/failure. We assume that 100 failures have been experienced. Using the **Logarithmic Poisson Model** (Musa–Okumoto), calculate
  i.   Current Intensity
  ii.   Decrement of failure intensity/ failure
  iii. Number of failures experienced for the logarithmic poisson model at 50 CPU hours of execution

6   Software Testing

6.1 INTRODUCTION

Software testing is a critical phase in the software development lifecycle. While we expect software to be error-free and responsive, it is crucial to note that launching software without proper testing can lead to higher costs in the long run, especially in systems where human safety is involved. Discovering and correcting errors early in the development process significantly reduces the cost of their removal.

It is also difficult for developers to reliably find errors in **their own** code. Therefore, many organizations assign testing responsibilities to a **separate, independent test team**. A common working definition is:

"Software testing is the process of executing a program with the intent of finding errors."

Exhaustive testing of all possible inputs is usually impossible. For example, a program that accepts **three 8-bit integers** as input has:

$$(2^8) \times (2^8) \times (2^8) = 256^3$$

different input combinations. Testing all such combinations would require an impractical amount of time. Therefore, designing an **effective but minimal set of test cases** is essential.

6.1.1   SOFTWARE TESTING: TERMINOLOGIES

Test Case and Test Suite

A **test case** specifies:

1. The **input data** (or initial conditions) to be supplied to the software, and

2. The **expected output** or observable behaviour.

When the actual output matches the expected output, the test case is said to have **passed**; otherwise, it **fails**.

A **test suite** is a set of test cases designed together to test a particular module, subsystem, or the system as a whole.

(Fields usually include: Test Case ID, Title/Objective, Preconditions, Input Data, Steps, Expected Result, Actual Result, Status, and Remarks.) A typical test case template is shown in Figure 47.

Test Case ID	Description	Pre-Condition	Procedure	Inputs	Expected Output	Post Conditions	Test Date	Result

Figure 46: Sample Test Case Template

6.2 TESTING STRATEGY

Testing does not happen at a single level. It is carried out in stages, beginning with individual components and gradually progressing to the entire system. Broadly, we can distinguish four main levels of testing:

1. **Unit Testing**
2. **Integration Testing**
3. **System Testing**
4. **Acceptance Testing**

In this section, we focus on the first two: **unit testing** and **integration testing**.

6.2.1   UNIT TESTING:

Unit testing focuses on verifying individual program units or modules (functions, classes, procedures). It is usually performed by the developer and checks whether each module:

- Works correctly **within its own boundary**, and
- Produces correct results for both **valid** and **invalid** inputs.

Unit testing often runs in **parallel** for multiple components, since units can be tested independently.

Unit test strategy is illustrated in Figure 48.

Figure 47: Unit Testing Workflow

Typical checks in unit testing include:

- **Module interface**
  - Verify that parameters and return values are passed correctly.
  - Ensure that data flows properly into and out of the unit.

- **Local data structures**
  - Confirm that temporary data retains integrity and is used correctly throughout the algorithm.

- **Control structure paths**
  - Exercise all **independent paths** in the unit so that each statement is executed at least once.

- **Boundary conditions**
  - Test extreme and edge values of inputs.
  - Many software failures occur at boundaries (e.g., minimum/maximum values, empty lists, zero, negative numbers).

- **Error-handling paths**
  - Force error conditions and verify that the module responds as specified (proper messages, safe recovery, no crashes).

If **data does not enter or leave** a module correctly, there is no point in further testing its internal logic—interface testing is therefore a natural first step.

Well-designed units (high cohesion, low coupling) are **easier to test**, and unit testing helps detect:

- Boundary errors
- Control flow errors
- Data structure and local variable errors

Drivers and Stubs

Because units are not stand-alone programs, **driver** and **stub** programs are often needed.

- **Driver**
  - A dummy "main" program that **calls** the unit under test, supplies test data, and records outputs.
  - Used when we test **lower-level** modules whose callers are not yet implemented.

- **Stub**
  - A dummy subprogram that **replaces** a called lower-level module.
  - It usually does minimal data manipulation, prints a simple message, and returns control to the caller.
  - Used in **top-down** testing when lower-level modules are not yet available.

Drivers and stubs are part of the **testing overhead** and should be kept as simple as possible. If appropriate drivers or stubs cannot be constructed, full testing of that unit may be postponed until the **integration testing** stage.

6.2.2   INTEGRATION TESTING

After unit testing, **integration testing** verifies that **individually tested modules work correctly together**. The goal is to expose errors arising from:

- Incorrect or inconsistent **interfaces**

- Wrong **data formats** or parameter passing

- Incorrect **control flow** or invocation order

- Assumptions about another module's behaviour

Integration testing thus focuses on **building the software architecture** incrementally and validating the interactions between components.

6.2.3   WHY INTEGRATION TESTING IS IMPORTANT:

- If we skip integration testing and only test the **entire system at once**, failures become **hard to localise**.
- In a large system with many modules, finding **which module or interface** caused a failure can be extremely time-consuming without structured integration testing.
- Integration testing provides a **stepwise approach**: once a small cluster of modules passes integration tests, we gain confidence and move to larger assemblies.

6.2.4 APPROACHES TO INTEGRATION TESTING:

We may use Top-down or bottom-up integration for construction of software architecture and testing.

a) **Top-Down Integration Testing**:

- In this approach, modules are integrated starting from the top of the control hierarchy (the main module) and moving downward. Subordinate modules are incorporated one at a time.

- Initially, low-level modules may not be available for testing, so they are replaced by **stubs**—dummy modules that simulate the behaviour of the lower-level modules.

- As testing progresses, the stubs are replaced with actual modules, and further testing is conducted.

Advantages:

- Testing of high-level logic and data flow occurs early.
- Major design flaws in the control structure are identified early.

Disadvantages:

- Stubs need to be created, which adds to the overhead.
- Low-level modules are tested later in the process, which may delay the detection of defects in them.

b) **Bottom-Up Integration Testing**:

- In bottom-up integration, testing starts from the lowest-level atomic modules and progresses upward in the hierarchy.

- As modules are integrated, **drivers** (simple programs that simulate higher-level control logic) are used to pass test data to the integrated lower-level modules.

- Drivers are gradually replaced by real modules as testing proceeds.

Advantages:

- No need for stubs, as real modules are tested early.
- Low-level functions are tested early, allowing for early detection of fundamental defects.

Disadvantages:

- High-level control and overall system behaviour are exercised late in the process.
- Design flaws or integration issues involving many subsystems might be discovered later, increasing rework.

Regression Testing:

Whenever modules are integrated or changed, there is a risk that previously working functionality may **break**. **Regression testing** addresses this risk.

- **Regression testing** is the process of **re-executing previously run test cases** to verify that modifications (bug fixes, new features, refactoring, or new integrations) have **not introduced new defects** into already tested parts of the software.

- It is especially important during integration testing, because new or changed modules can affect existing interfaces, shared data, or control flow.

In practice:

- A **regression test suite** is maintained and expanded over time.

- After each integration step or significant code change, relevant parts of the regression suite are rerun.

- Automated regression testing (e.g., via unit test frameworks and CI pipelines) is widely used in modern software projects.

6.2.5   SYSTEM TESTING

System testing evaluates the entire software system by integrating all the modules and components in a complete working environment. The purpose of system testing is to ensure that the software meets both **functional** and **non-functional requirements** as specified by the client or stakeholders. System testing is the final testing stage before the software is delivered to the end-user.

System testing involves a variety of testing methods that cover the system's performance, security, functionality, and scalability. It ensures that the integrated system functions correctly in real-world scenarios.

<u>Types of System Testing</u>:

In practice, system testing is an umbrella term that includes several specialised test types, such as security, performance, load, and stress testing.

(a) **Security Testing-** Security testing ensures that the software is protected against unauthorized access or security breaches. For systems handling sensitive data, it is crucial to safeguard the system from any potential threats that could lead to data leaks, system hijacking, or other security vulnerabilities.

Key Requirements:

- **Integrity and Authentication**: Ensures that data is secure and can only be accessed by authorized users.

- **Access Control**: Prevents unauthorized users from gaining access to sensitive information.

- **Confidentiality**: Ensures that information is delivered only to the intended recipient.

- **Reliability**: Verifies that the system has low chances of failure and can recover in case of a breach or failure.

Security Testing Activities:

During security testing, the tester plays the role(s) of the individual who desires to penetrate the system

- Attempt to gain unauthorized access by exploiting weak passwords or vulnerabilities.

- Overload the system to deny services to legitimate users (e.g., **DoS** attacks).

- Simulate system recovery from intentional failures to test for resilience.

- Browse through insecure data to identify potential security gaps.

The role of the system designer is to make penetration cost more than the value of the information that will be obtained.

(b) Performance Testing- The goal of performance testing is to evaluate how well the system performs under various conditions. For real-time systems, performance is critical, and failure to meet performance criteria can lead to system rejection. Performance testing is conducted throughout the testing process but is especially crucial after system integration. The following issues must be addressed during performance testing:

1. Performance of the system during peak hours (response time, reliability and availability).
2. Points at which the system performance degrades or system fails.
3. Impact of the degraded performance on the customer satisfaction and retention.

(c) Load Testing -   Load testing simulates multiple users accessing the system simultaneously to evaluate its behavior under heavy workloads. It helps assess whether the system can handle the expected user load without crashing or becoming unresponsive.

Load testing is particularly important for web applications and large-scale enterprise systems where high traffic is expected.

(d) Stress Testing - Stress tests are designed to confront programs with abnormal situations. *Stress testing* executes a system in a manner that demands resources in abnormal quantity, frequency, or volume.

Unlike performance and load testing, stress testing evaluates the response of the system when the system is given a load beyond its specified limits. It is also used to monitor and check the reliability of an application when available resources are on beyond maximum usage. Essentially, the tester attempts to break the program.

Examples of Stress Testing:

- Increasing input data rates beyond expected levels.

- Running tests that consume maximum system memory or other resources.

- Observing how the system recovers after encountering abnormal resource usage.

6.2.6   ACCEPTANCE TESTING

Acceptance testing is the final phase of testing conducted to determine whether the software meets the business and functional requirements defined by the customer or end-user. It serves as the last validation checkpoint before the software is deployed into production. The primary goal of acceptance testing is to validate that the software performs as intended in real-world scenarios and is ready for operational use.

Types of Acceptance Testing:

a) **Alpha Testing**: Alpha testing is carried out at the developer's site by internal teams or select potential users. It is typically conducted in a controlled environment and focuses on finding bugs or defects that were not detected during earlier testing phases.

Alpha testing occurs during the later stages of development but before the software is released to a wider audience.

Alpha testing often simulates real-world scenarios to identify functionality issues, performance bottlenecks, or usability concerns. It is specifically aimed at finding bugs before the public release.

b) **Beta Testing**: Beta testing is performed by real users in an uncontrolled, live environment.

Beta Testing

- Conducted at the **customer's or end user's environment**.

- Involves real users working with the software in **uncontrolled, live conditions**.

- The development team usually has limited or indirect presence.

Beta testing:

- Reveals issues that only arise under diverse, real-world operational conditions.

- Collects feedback on functionality, usability, performance, and overall user satisfaction.

- Provides input for final refinements before the official product release.

Example: Companies like Microsoft often conducts beta testing for new versions of its software, such as Windows or Office, allowing thousands of users to provide feedback before the official launch.

6.2.7   DEPLOYMENT TESTING -

Deployment testing, sometimes referred to as **configuration testing**, ensures that the software can be successfully installed and configured in its target environment. This type of testing is essential for verifying that the software functions correctly on various platforms, networks, and operating systems. Deployment testing is often performed after acceptance testing and before the software is released to end-users.

Key Focus Areas in Deployment Testing:

- **Installation Procedures**: Deployment testing evaluates the accuracy and reliability of installation processes. It verifies whether the software can be properly installed, configured, and uninstalled in the target environments.

- **Platform Compatibility**: The software must be tested on different hardware, operating systems, and network configurations to ensure it operates as expected across various environments. This includes testing on different browsers, mobile devices, servers, and databases, if applicable.

- **Configuration Testing**: Deployment testing also focuses on how the software behaves when running under different configurations. This includes adjusting parameters such as memory, disk space, and processing power to ensure that the software adapts to varying conditions.

- **Documentation and User Support**: In addition to testing the software itself, deployment testing ensures that installation guides, configuration manuals, and user support documentation are accurate, clear, and helpful for end-users during the deployment process.

Deployment testing gives confidence that the system will work correctly in the customer's environment, not just in the developer's lab.

6.3 INTERNAL AND EXTERNAL VIEWS OF TESTING

Software can be tested from two complementary perspectives:

1. **External view** – Black-box / functional testing
2. **Internal view** – White-box / structural testing

Using both views together leads to more thorough and effective testing.

6.3.1 EXTERNAL VIEW (BLACK-BOX / FUNCTIONAL TESTING):

Black-box testing focuses on evaluating the software's functionality without considering its internal structure. In **black-box testing**, the tester treats the software as a "black box":

- Internal implementation details are **ignored**.
- Tests are designed from **requirements**, **use cases**, and **interfaces**, not from the code.

The tester supplies inputs and observes outputs, checking whether the behaviour matches the specification.

Advantages:

- No need to understand the internal code or design.

- Strong focus on verifying that **user-visible behaviour** and **functional requirements** are met.

- Useful for testing complete subsystems and systems, including user interfaces and APIs.

Typical questions:

- Are all specified functions available and working correctly?

- Does the software correctly validate and process input and generate the correct output?

- Does the system behave as expected in normal, boundary, and error conditions from a user's perspective?

6.3.2 INTERNAL VIEW (WHITE-BOX / STRUCTURAL TESTING):

White-box testing involves examining the internal structure of the software. In **white-box testing**, the tester has access to the **internal structure and code** of the software. Test cases are derived from the program's logic, control flow, and data structures.

The goal is to ensure that:
- All important internal paths and conditions have been exercised, and
- The implementation is correct and robust.

Advantages:
- Helps detect logic errors, unreachable code, incorrect conditions, and boundary issues in loops.
- Enables measurement of structural coverage (e.g., statement, branch, path coverage).

Key focus areas:
- Are all significant code paths executed at least once?

- Are decisions and loops tested for typical, boundary, and exceptional cases?

- Are internal data structures (arrays, pointers, collections, etc.) used safely and consistently?

In practice, **black-box** and **white-box** testing are not alternatives but **complements**:

- Black-box testing validates that the system does **the right things** (correct external behaviour).

- White-box testing validates that the system does things in the **right way** (correct internal implementation).

6.3.3 FUNCTIONAL TESTING

Functional testing (also called **black-box testing** or **behavioural testing**) focuses on the *external behaviour* of the software. The tester supplies inputs and checks outputs against the specification, without considering how the outputs are produced internally.

The aim is to validate that the software:

- Implements all specified functions correctly.
- Handles valid and invalid inputs properly.
- Interacts correctly with files, databases, and external interfaces.

Black-box testing typically aims to uncover errors in:

1. Incorrect or missing functions.
2. Interface errors.
3. Data structure or external database access errors.
4. Behaviour or performance errors.
5. Initialisation and termination errors.

Black-box testing **complements** white-box testing; it is usually applied in later stages (system and acceptance testing), whereas white-box techniques are often used earlier at unit or component level. Plenty of black-box test design techniques exist as shown in Figure 49.

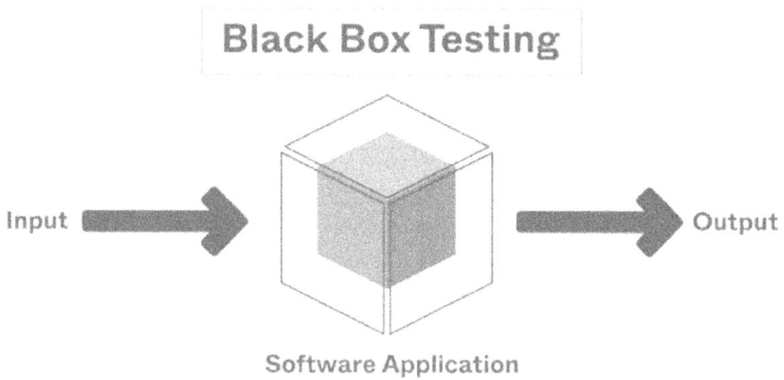

Figure 48: Black -Box Testing

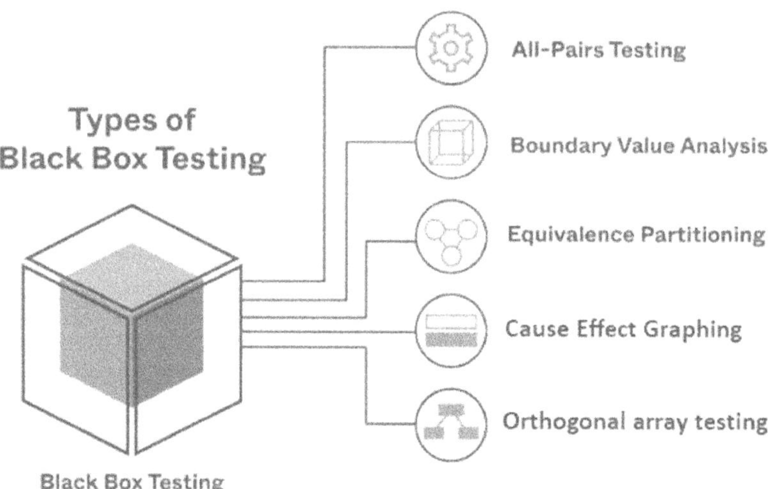

Figure 49: Types of black bog testing

Functional Testing Techniques:

A variety of techniques are used in functional testing to ensure all aspects of the system are thoroughly examined.

6.3.3.1 *Boundary Value Analysis*

Boundary Value Analysis (BVA) is a black-box testing technique that involves testing the boundary values of input variables. It assumes that errors often occur at the boundaries rather than in the middle of the input range.

For instance, if an input variable is supposed to accept values between a and b, boundary value testing involves testing the values a, b, and the values just above and below these limits.

If a function F has two input variables x and y with the valid ranges:

$$a \leq x \leq b, \quad c \leq y \leq d$$

then typical boundary test cases include values at and just inside the boundaries, such as:

$$(a,c), (a,d), (b,c) \text{ and } (b.d)$$

These boundary values will help determine how the system behaves at the limits of valid input ranges. (Figure 50) help verify the behaviour at the edges of the valid input domain.

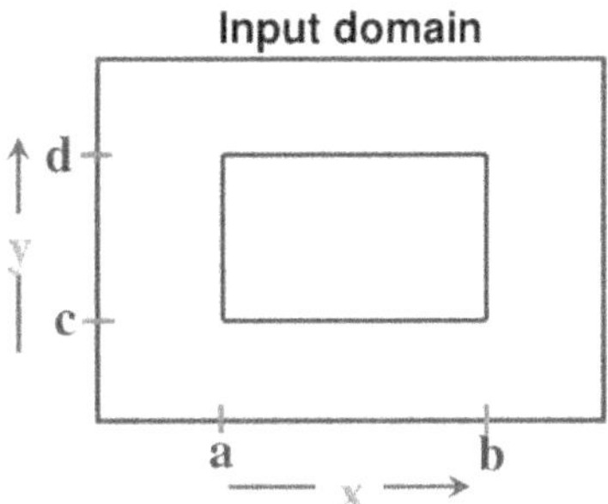

Figure 50:Input domain for a function of x, y in boundary value analysis

6.3.3.2 Robustness Testing

Robustness Testing extends BVA by checking how the system behaves when inputs slightly exceed their valid ranges. The objective is to ensure the system handles invalid or extreme input values gracefully without crashing.

Example: For the function F described earlier, robustness testing involves testing the values just beyond the boundaries, such as:

(a-1, c-1), (a-1, c), (a-1, c+1), (a-1, d-1) ....and so on

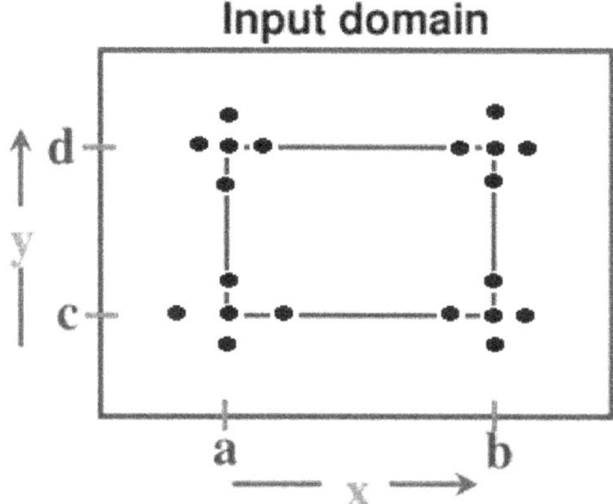

Figure 51: Input domain for two variables x and y in robustness testing

This helps identify how well the system copes with out-of-range inputs.

6.3.3.3 Equivalence Class Partitioning

In **Equivalence Class Testing**, input data is partitioned into classes where the system behaves similarly. The idea is to minimize the number of test cases by selecting representative values from each class rather than testing every possible value. If one value from an equivalence class leads to an error, all other values in the same class are also likely to fail.

For each class test cases may be taken at boundary values.

Example: if an input condition takes values from 1 to 999. Then one of class will be with values less than 1, other between 1 to 999 and third with values >999

Boundary Value Analysis often complements equivalence partitioning by choosing representatives *at or near* the class boundaries (e.g. 0, 1, 999, 1000).

6.3.3.4 Decision Table Testing

Decision Table Testing is a technique used when the output of a system depends on multiple input conditions. It creates a table to represent different combinations of inputs and the corresponding outputs.

This approach helps ensure that all combinations of input conditions are covered during testing. Table 10 shows an example of decision table for email login module

Table 10: Decision table for login module

Email	T	T	F	F
Password	T	F	T	F
Action/ Outcome	Account Page	Incorrect Password	Incorrect Email	Incorrect Credentials

Each combination of inputs is tested to verify that the system behaves correctly.

6.3.3.5 Cause Effect Graphing

Boundary value and equivalence partitioning does not consider combination of input circumstances. If we consider all possible combinations of an equivalence then it will lead a large set of test cases, which may in turn became impractical to test. e.g. for n inputs we have 2^n combinations.

Cause-Effect Graphing is a systematic method of deriving test cases by modeling input conditions (causes) and their corresponding outputs (effects). It helps visualize and organize complex test cases that involve multiple input combinations.

- **Causes** – input conditions or events.
- **Effects** – resulting outputs or system behaviours.

Steps involved in generation of test cases under this method are

1. **Identify Causes and Effects**: Causes represent distinct input conditions, and effects represent the resulting output or system behavior.

2. **Assign Unique Numbers**: Each cause and effect is given a unique identifier.

3. **Design Cause-Effect Graph**: A graph is created to represent the relationships between causes and effects.

4. **Define Constraints**: Any constraints or dependencies between causes and effects are added.

5. **Create Decision Table**: A decision table is generated based on the graph to guide the creation of test cases.

6.3.4 STRUCTURAL TESTING

Structural testing (also called **white-box or glass-box testing)** validates the internal logic of the software. The tester uses knowledge of the program's structure to design test cases.

Using white-box testing methods, you can derive test cases that aims to-

1. Exercise all **independent paths** within a module at least once.
2. Exercise all **decision outcomes** (true and false).

3. Execute **loops** at their boundaries and within operational ranges.,

4. Exercise **internal data structures** (arrays, pointers, lists, etc.) to ensure integrity.

Key techniques include path testing, control-flow graph analysis, cyclomatic complexity, and data-flow testing.

6.3.4.1 Path Testing

Path Testing is the name given to a group of test techniques based on judiciously selecting a set of test paths through the program. It is a structural testing technique where the source code is required for the generation of test cases. This type of testing involves:

- Generate a set of paths that will cover every branch in the program
- Find a set of test cases that will execute every path out of program paths

6.3.4.2 Control Flow Graph (CFG):

Control flow of a program can be analyzed using a Control Flow Graph. Draw the corresponding control flow graph of the program in which all the executable paths are to be discovered.

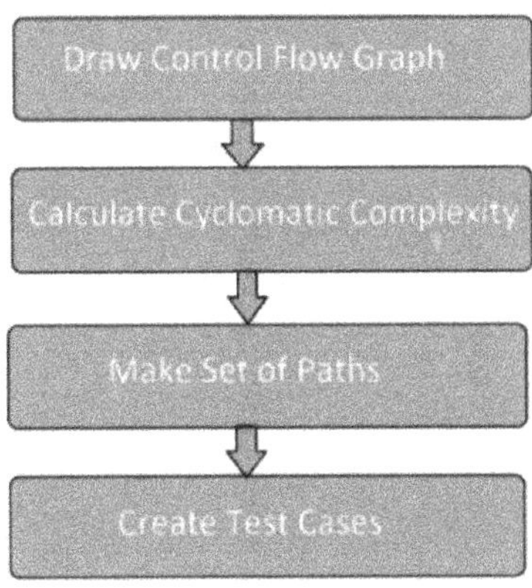

Figure 52: Path testing process

The flow graph is a directed graph in which nodes are either statements or of a statement and edges represent flow of control.

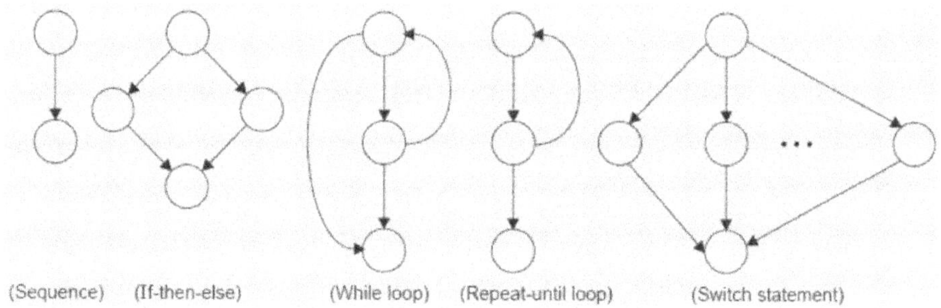

Figure 53:Basic Components of control flow graph

6.3.4.3 *Cyclomatic Complexity:*

Cyclomatic Complexity is a metric used to measure the complexity of a program by counting the number of independent paths through the code. It provides an estimate of how many test cases are needed for complete path coverage.

The formula for calculating McCabe's Cyclomatic Complexity is:

$$V(G) = E - N + 2P$$

Where,

- E = Number of edges in control flow graph
- N = Number of vertices in control flow graph
- P = No of Connected Components

(In case the main program has multiple subroutines, flow graph of these subroutines may result in more than one connected component)

Properties of Cyclomatic Complexity:

- $V(G) \geq 1$

- V (G) = number of independent paths in program/module
- V (G) = no of regions in graph (including outer region)

Steps to Compute Cyclomatic Complexity:

- **Draw the Control Flow Graph:** A flow graph is a directed graph where nodes represent code segments and edges represent control flow transitions.
- **Count the Edges (E) and Nodes (N).**
- **Apply the Formula to** compute the cyclomatic complexity V (G).
- **Determine Independent Paths:** The complexity number gives the number of independent paths that need to be tested.

Create Test Cases: Create test case for each path of the set obtained in above step.

Advantages of Path Testing:

- Reduces the redundant tests.
- Focuses on the logic of the programs.
- Used in test case design.

Example 6.1: Program to check whether the sum of two integers is positive, negative, or zero.

```
#include <stdio.h>
#include <conio.h>
int main ()
{
int a, b, sum;
printf ("Enter value of First Number: ");
scanf ("%d", &a);
printf ("Enter value of Second Number: ");
scanf ("%d", &b);
sum = a+b;
if (sum < 0) {
printf ("Sum of two numbers is Negative ");
} else if (sum==0) {
printf ("Sum of two numbers is Zero or Neutral");
} else {
```

```
printf ("Sum of two numbers is Positive");
}
}
```

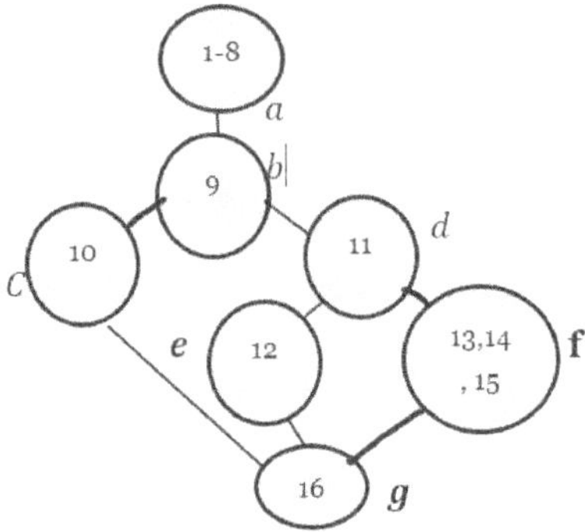

Figure 54: Program and Flow Graph for Example 6.1

The Value of cyclomatic complexity for control flow graph in Figure 54 can be calculated as:

$$V (G) = 8\text{-}7\text{+}2(1) = 3$$

Here, e= 8, n =7 and P=1

There will be 3 independent paths in the graph

- Path 1: $a \rightarrow b \rightarrow c \rightarrow g$(sum < 0 branch)
- Path 2: $a \rightarrow b \rightarrow d \rightarrow e \rightarrow g$(sum == 0 branch)
- Path 3: $a \rightarrow b \rightarrow d \rightarrow f \rightarrow g$(sum > 0 branch)

At least three test cases are needed to exercise each outcome:

- sum < 0 (e.g. a = −5, b = −2)
- sum == 0 (e.g. a = 5, b = −5)
- sum > 0 (e.g. a = 3, b = 4)

6.3.4.4 *Data flow Testing*

Data Flow Testing is a type of structural testing. It is a method that is used to find the test paths of a program according to the locations of definitions and uses of variables in the program. It has nothing to do with data flow diagrams. It is concerned with:

- Statements where variables receive values,
- Statements where these values are used or referenced.

To illustrate the approach of data flow testing, assume that each statement in the program assigned a unique statement number. For a statement number S-

DEF(S) = {X | statement S contains the definition of X}

USE(S) = {X | statement S contains the use of X}

If a statement is a loop or if condition then its DEF set is empty and USE set is based on the condition of statement s.

Data Flow Testing uses the control flow graph to find the situations that can interrupt the flow of the program.

Reference or define anomalies in the flow of the data are detected at the time of associations between values and variables. These anomalies are:

- A variable is defined but not used or referenced,
- A variable is used but never defined,
- A variable is defined twice before it is used

Usage and advantages of Data Flow Testing:

- To find a variable that is used but never defined,
- To find a variable that is defined but never used,
- To find a variable that is defined multiple times before it is use,
- Deallocating a variable before it is used.

Disadvantages of Data Flow Testing
- Time consuming and costly process
- Requires knowledge of programming languages

This helps ensure that variables are properly defined before use and that all definitions eventually contribute to useful computation.

Example 6.2:

```
1. read x, y;
2. if(x>y)
3. a = x+1
else
4. a = y-1
5. print a;
```

Control flow graph of above example:

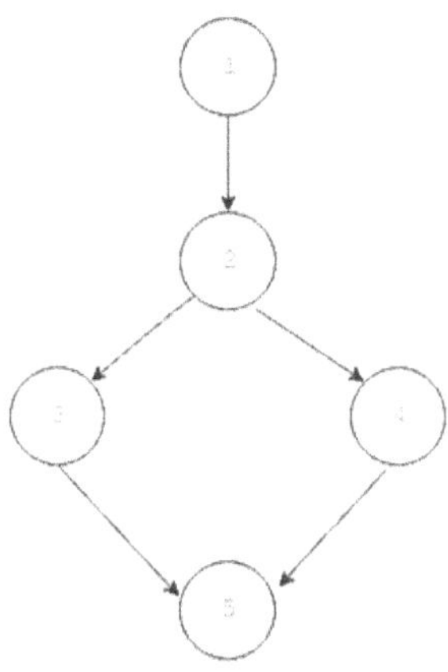

Figure 55: Control Flow Graph

Define/use of variables of above example: Table 11

Variable	Defined at node	Used at node
x	1	2, 3
y	1	2, 4
a	3, 4	5

6.3.5   MUTATION TESTING

Richard Lipton proposed the mutation testing in 1971 for the first time. **Mutation Testing** is a type of Software Testing that is performed to design new software tests and also evaluate the quality of already existing software tests. (Jia & Harman, 2011)

Mutation testing is related to modification a program in small ways. It focuses to help the tester develop effective tests or locate weaknesses in the test data used for the program. Although high cost reduced the use of mutation testing but now it is widely used for languages such as Java and XML.

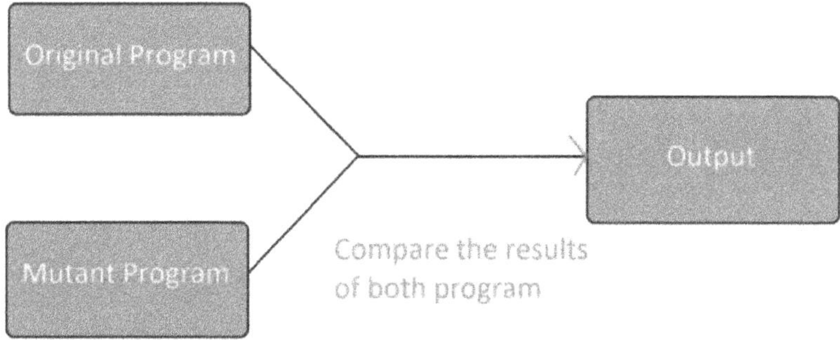

Figure 56: Mutation Testing

Mutation testing can be applied to design models, specifications, databases, tests, and XML. It is a **structural testing** technique because it uses the internal structure of the program to guide testing.

Objective of Mutation Testing:
- To identify pieces of code that are not tested properly.
- To identify hidden defects that can't be detected using other testing methods.
- To discover new kinds of errors or bugs.
- To calculate the mutation score.
- Study **error propagation** and **state infection** in the program.
- To assess the quality of the test cases.

Types of Mutation Testing:

Mutation testing is basically of 3 types:

1. **Value Mutations**:

    In this type of testing the values (of some constants) are changed to detect errors in the program. Basically, a small value is changed to a larger value or a larger value is changed to a smaller value.

Example:

```
Initial Code:
int mod = 1000000007;
int a = 12345678;
int b = 98765432;
int c = (a + b) % mod;

Mutated Code:
int mod = 1007;
int a = 12345678;
int b = 98765432;
int c = (a + b) % mod;
```

2. Decision Mutations:

In decisions mutations are logical or arithmetic operators are changed to detect errors in the program.

```
Example:
Initial Code:
if(a < b)
 c = 10;
else
 c = 20;

Mutated Code:
if(a > b)
 c = 10;
else
 c = 20;
```

3. Statement Mutations:

In statement mutations a statement is deleted or it is replaced by some other statement.

Example:

```
Initial Code:
if(a < b)
 c = 10;
else
 c = 20;

Mutated Code:
if(a < b)
 d = 10;
else
 d = 20;
```

Tools used for Mutation Testing:

Some commonly used mutation testing tools are:

- **Judy**
- **Jester**
- **Jumble**
- **PIT**
- **MuClipse**

Advantages

- Achieves a **high level of error detection**.
- Helps uncover **ambiguities** and weaknesses in the source code.
- Exposes **loopholes** and untested branches.
- Encourages testers to design **stronger, more thorough test cases**.
- Leads to **better quality code** and improved fault tolerance.

Disadvantages

- Computationally **expensive and time-consuming**, as many mutants must be generated and tested.

- Some mutants are **complex and difficult to interpret**.

- Requires testers with **good programming skills**.

- Choosing an appropriate **automation tool** is critical and non-trivial.

6.4 DEBUGGING

Debugging is the process of identifying, analyzing, and fixing bugs or defects within a software program. Unlike testing, which aims to identify errors, debugging focuses on isolating the exact source of the error and correcting it.

Goal of Testing is to identify errors. Testing will give symptoms of presence of error. After that we are to investigate for source of error. i.e. first identify module than section. This is called as debugging.

"Activity of locating & correcting errors"

Effective debugging is crucial for delivering a reliable and error-free software product. The process may be started once a failure has detected. It is often considered one of the most challenging and time-consuming tasks in software development, as it requires both technical skill and analytical thinking.

Characteristics of Bugs

- **Distributed Causes:** Symptom and cause may be geographically different
- Geographic Separation of Symptom and Cause: The place where an error manifest (symptom) may be far removed from where the bug actually exists in the code (cause).
- Disappearing Symptoms: Sometimes, fixing one bug may temporarily mask or eliminate the symptoms of another bug, creating the illusion that it has been resolved.

- Symptoms may be caused by a human error (not easy to trace)
- Difficult to retrace or reproduce (where input ordering is indeterminate)

6.4.1 DEBUGGING APPROACHES

1. **Core Dumps and Memory Dumps**
   Memory dumps of all registers and location Disadvantage: Complex as large data and in form of HEX numbers

2. **Tracing and Logging:**
   Tracing involves recording a history of function calls or execution flow leading up to the error. Logs are statements inserted in the code to record variable states, decision points, and function entries and exits.

3. **Print Statements**
   A simple and widely used method, print statements help track variable values and execution flow by displaying them on the console.

4. **Automated Debugging Tools:**
   Modern (IDEs and standalone debuggers (e.g. GDB, JDB) offer debugging tools that allow developers to set breakpoints, step through code, inspect variables, and analyze call stacks. e.g. GNU Debugger, JDB (Java Debugger).

6.4.2 DEBUGGING PROCESS

The debugging process generally consists of three main steps:

1. **Identify the Bug:**

- o This involves confirming the presence of a bug. It often starts with analyzing the error messages, logs, and core dumps to locate where the bug might be.

- o Tools and techniques like print statements, logging, or trace analysis can help during this phase.

2. **Isolate the Bug:**

- o Once the bug is identified, isolating it involves narrowing down the specific module, function, or line of code causing the error. This include setting breakpoints, examining the call stack, and inspecting variable values.

3. **Fix and Validate:**

- o After identifying, the next step is to modify the code to correct it. Post-fix, the solution is validated by re-running the test cases and ensuring that the error has been resolved without introducing new issues.

A deep understanding of the debugging process and adherence to best practices can significantly improve software quality and reliability.

6.5 VERIFICATION AND VALIDATION

Verification and Validation (V&V) are critical processes in software engineering aimed at ensuring that the developed software meets both the specified requirements and the intended purpose. These processes help to establish the software's quality and ensure it functions as expected, minimizing the risk of defects and increasing reliability.

Testing = Verification+ Validation

Validation is something that you do at the end of software development or system development. You may have your own software or system developed ready in place and you want to be able to check if the software of system meets all its requirements when you do that at the end of the development then that is what is called validation.

"Are we the building the right product?"

Validation involves executing the software to uncover any issues that affect functionality, usability, or performance. It includes, activities like functional testing, Performance testing, regression testing etc.

Verification deals with what you test or verify while developing software. So, while developing software you might go through various phases, phase where you define requirements, phase where you do design and architecture. Verification is a process of evaluating a system or component to determine whether the product of a given development phase satisfy the conditions imposed at the start of that phase.

"Are we building the product right".

Verification involves various static techniques, like Requirements Verification, Design Verification, Code Review and Analysis, code inspections and walkthroughs and Documentation Verification

Examples:
- **Requirements verification** – completeness, consistency, clarity of SRS.
- **Design verification** – architectural and detailed design consistency with requirements.
- **Code verification** – adherence to coding standards, reviews, static analysis.
- **Documentation verification** – correctness and clarity of manuals and specifications.

Verification is heavily based on **static techniques**:
- Reviews and walkthroughs
- Inspections

- Static analysis tools

Well-defined V&V activities, aligned with relevant standards, improve software quality, reduce risk, and increase user satisfaction.

6.6 TESTING TOOLS AND STANDARDS

One way to improve the quality & quantity of testing is to make the process as simple as possible for the tester. This means that tools should be as concise, powerful and easy to use as possible.

Tools and standards help make testing **more efficient, systematic, and repeatable**.

- **Testing tools** support automation, test execution, reporting, and environment simulation.

- **Testing standards** define terminology, processes, and best practices.

Together, they help teams deliver robust and reliable software.

6.6.1   TYPES OF TESTING TOOLS

Broadly categorized as static and dynamic tools:

- ✓ **Static Test Tools**
    - ✓ Seek support of static testing
    - ✓ Does not require actual execution
    - ✓ These tools do not involve actual input and output

    Common types:

    A. **Flow analyzers:** They ensure consistency in data flow from input to output
    B. **Path tester:** They find unused code and code with contradictions.

C. **Coverage Analyzers:** It ensures that all logic paths are tested.

D. **Interface Analyzers:** It examines the effects of passing variables and data between modules.

✓ **Dynamic Test Tools**

Dynamic testing tools are used during the execution of the software.

    ✓ Seek support of dynamic testing
    ✓ Require actual testing

Common types:

A. **Test driver:** It inputs data into a module-under-test

B. **Test Beds:** Test beds often include simulators to create a realistic test environment, especially for embedded systems or IoT applications. It simultaneously displays source code along with program under execution

C. **Emulators:** response facilities are used to emulate parts of the system not yet developed. Emulators are commonly used in mobile and embedded software testing.

D. **Mutation analyzers:** inject faults (mutants) into code and evaluate the strength of the test suite.

6.6.2 COMMON TESTING TOOLS BY CATEGORY

Here are some commonly used testing tools, categorized by their specific use case:

- **Functional Testing:** Selenium, QTP (QuickTest Professional), TestComplete

- **Performance Testing:** LoadRunner, JMeter, NeoLoad

- **Unit Testing:** JUnit, NUnit, TestNG, PyTest

- **Security Testing:** OWASP ZAP, Burp Suite, Veracode

- **Continuous Integration/Continuous Delivery (CI/CD):** Jenkins, Bamboo, CircleCI

- **Bug Tracking and Test Management:** Jira, Bugzilla, TestRail, HP ALM (Application Lifecycle Management)

Each of these tools offers unique features that support various testing activities, and their selection often depends on the testing requirements, and the team's familiarity with the tools. The choice of tool depends on technology stack, project scale, process maturity, and team expertise.

6.6.3　TESTING STANDARDS

Testing standards provide guidelines and best practices for conducting software testing, ensuring consistency, reliability, and quality. Adherence to these standards helps create a common understanding of testing processes across teams and organizations.

Important families include:

- IEEE Standards: e.g. standards for test documentation, test processes, and terminology.
- ISO/IEC Standards:　e.g. ISO/IEC standards relating to software quality, testing processes, and life-cycle models.
- ISTQB (International Software Testing Qualifications Board): Provides globally recognised certification schemes and a common vocabulary for testing concepts and processes.

Both testing tools and standards are indispensable for delivering robust, reliable, and high-quality software that meets customer expectations and complies with industry regulations.

6.7 EXERCISES

2.1 What is Software Testing? What are the different levels of testing?

2.2 Why testing is important is software life cycle? Discuss Objectives of Testing.

2.3 Consider a program for the determination of the nature of the roots of a quadratic equation. Design the boundary value test cases for it.

2.4 What do you mean by regression testing?

2.5 Discuss the structural (White-Box) testing. How it is different from functional (Black-Box) testing?

2.6 Briefly discuss the following:
   i.   Test case design and test suite
   ii. Verification and Validation
   iii. Alpha, Beta and Acceptance testing

2.7 Differentiate between Unit Testing and Integration Testing. What are stubs and drivers?

2.8 Explain in detail about the term debugging. Describe the main steps in the debugging process.

7   SOFTWARE MAINTENANCE

Software maintenance is a crucial and broad activity that includes tasks such as correcting errors, enhancing capabilities, removing obsolete features, and optimizing the system for performance and efficiency. The goal is to ensure that the software remains functional, relevant, and efficient throughout its lifetime.

7.1 CATEGORIES OF MAINTENANCE

Software maintenance is commonly classified into four categories:

- ✓ **Corrective Maintenance**: refers to modifications initiated by identification of defects in the software as corrective measure
- ✓ **Adaptive maintenance**: Included modifying the software to match in the ever-changing environment. (e.g., new operating systems, hardware, or external regulations).
- ✓ **Perfective Maintenance:** It means improving processing efficiency or performance, or restructuring the software to improve changeability. This may include enhancement of existing system functionality, improvement in computational efficiency etc.
- ✓ **Preventive Maintenance:** regularly and routinely performed to reduce the chances of failure and unplanned downtime that can be very costly.

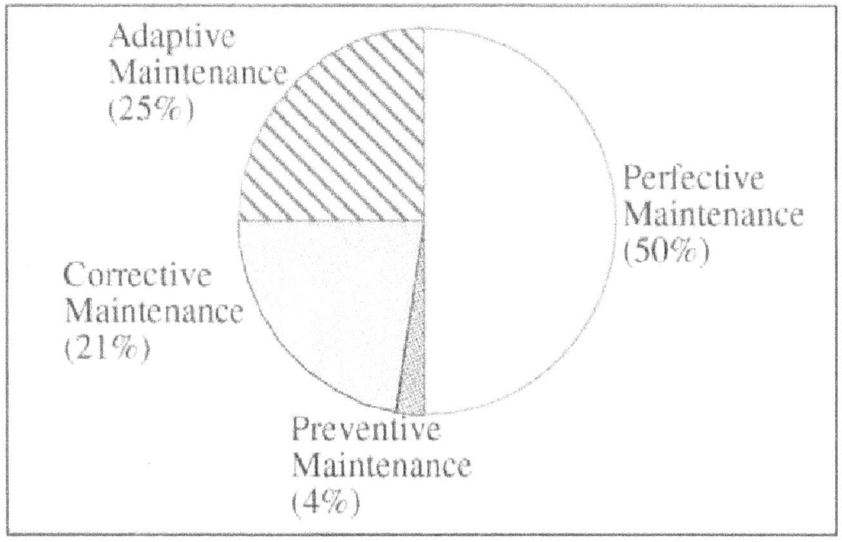

Figure 57 : Distribution of maintenance effort

7.2 MANAGEMENT OF MAINTENANCE!

A common misconception about maintenance is that it is not manageable. However, maintenance is a manageable task.

Challenges during Maintenance

- ➤ Often the program is written by a person different from the person who maintain/change it.
- ➤ Often the program is changed by person who did not understand it clearly as he/she has not written that code.
- ➤ Program listings are not structured.
- ➤ Systems are not suitable designed for changes.

In order to avoid and handle these challenges, software systems should be maintainable and kept flexible and adaptable for future changes, throughout the development process i.e., from specifications and design to coding and deployment. However, if we face these problems when maintenance process starts, we need to take some steps to resolve.

Possible Responses to Maintenance Challenges:

> ➤ **Budget and effort reallocation:** Ensuring adequate budget and resources are allocated to maintenance activities to avoid major system failures

> ➤ **Complete replacement of the system:** In some cases, it may be more cost-effective to replace the system entirely.

> ➤ **Maintenance of existing system:** Continuing to maintain the existing system while gradually enhancing its maintainability for future changes.

7.3 MAINTENANCE PROCESS

The **software maintenance process** is a broad set of activities, including error corrections, capability enhancements, removal of obsolete features, and optimizations. The process typically involves several stages:

1. **Identification of the Modification:**

   - Capture change requests (bugs, enhancements, environmental changes).

   - Define what needs to be modified and why.

2. **Impact Analysis:**

   - Analyzing how the changes will affect other parts of the system to minimize the ripple effect.

3. **Ripple Effect**

   - The third phase consists of accounting for all of the ripple effect as a consequence of program modifications.

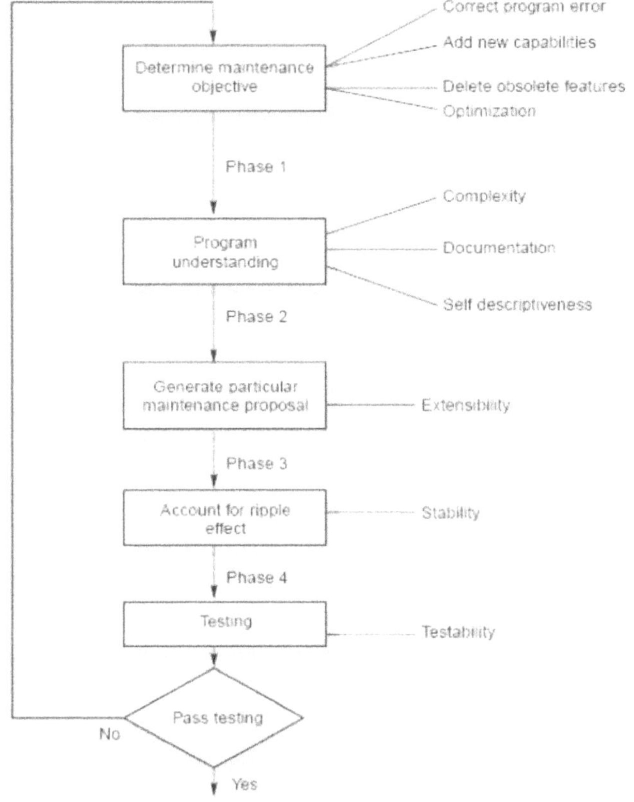

Figure 58: The software maintenance process

4. Modified Program Testing

- The fourth phase consists of testing the modified program to ensure that the modified program has at least the same reliability level as before.

7.4 MAINTENANCE MODELS

Several models provide structured approaches to manage and execute software maintenance effectively. These models help organize maintenance activities and facilitate a more systematic approach to addressing various maintenance requirements.

7.4.1 QUICK-FIX MODEL

This is an **ad-hoc approach** to maintenance, where changes are made quickly to address immediate issues. The problem is identified, fixed, and the system is recompiled for a new version.

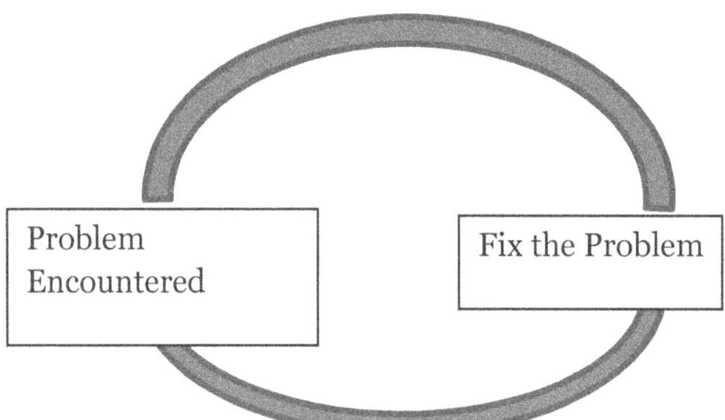

Figure 59: Quick Fix Maintenance Model

It's a reactive model, commonly used in urgent situations, but lacks a structured approach to long-term maintenance as shown in Figure 61.

7.4.2 ITERATIVE ENHANCEMENT MODEL

Originally proposed as a development model, the **Iterative Enhancement Model** fits maintenance very well.

Key ideas:

• Starts with the existing system's requirements, design, code, test, and analysis documents;

• Modifies the set of documents, starting with the highest-level document affected by the changes down through the full set of documents; and

• At each step of the evolutionary process, lets you redesign the system, based on analysis of the existing system.

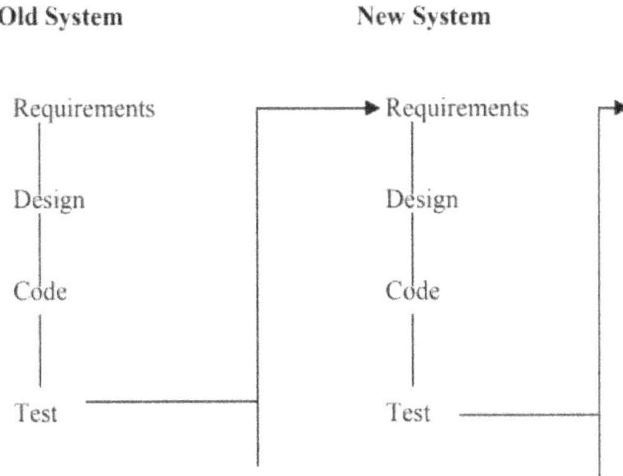

Figure 60: Iterative-enhancement model

This model:

- Encourages controlled and traceable evolution.

- Helps maintain consistency among requirements, design, code, and tests.

7.4.3   REUSE ORIENTED MODEL

In contrast to iterative enhancement model that starts with evaluation of the existing system, in reuse-based models, maintenance process starts with requirements analysis and design of new system, with the concept of reusing whatever requirements, design and code are available from the old system. Reuse models following major steps.

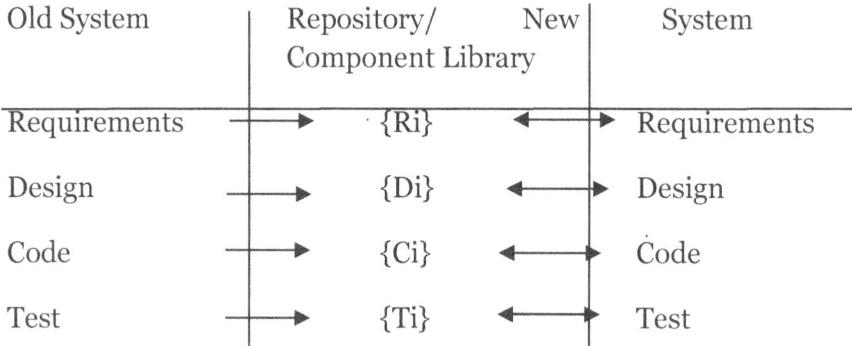

Instead of directly modifying the old system, we:

1. Perform **requirements analysis** for the *new* version of the system.

2. Identify reusable items from the old system:

    o   Requirements {Ri}, Design elements {Di}, Code components {Ci}, Test artefacts {Ti}

3. Assemble the new system using:

    o   Reused components where possible. New components where necessary.

This model encourages building a **component library/repository** to systematically reuse high-quality modules and designs.

7.4.4 BOEHM'S MAINTENANCE MODEL

In 1983, Barry Boehm proposed a model for the maintenance process which was based upon the economic models and principles. Economic decisions are a major building block of many processes and Boehm's Model could not only improve productivity in the maintenance but it also helps to understand the process very well.

Boehm maintenance process model represented as a **closed-loop cycle** as shown in the below diagram

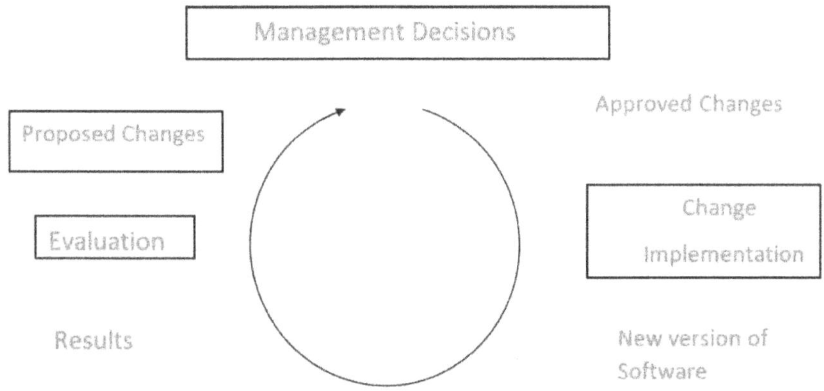

Figure 61: Boehm Maintenance Model

Key Aspects :

Boehm theorized that the process is primarily driven by management decisions, with these decisions shaping the direction of the process.

At this stage, necessary changes are identified through the application of specific strategies and cost-benefit analyses to a set of proposed modifications. The changes that are approved are backed by organizational budgets, which determine the scale and type of resources allocated.

Boehm recognized that the role of the maintenance manager is to balance and pursue the goals of maintenance while considering the constraints imposed by the operating environment. Consequently, the maintenance process should be guided by the decisions of the maintenance manager, who typically weighs objectives against constraints.

Boehm's Maintenance Cost Formula

Boehm also introduced a cost formula in the context of COCOMO, using the concept of **Annual Change Traffic (ACT)**, which is defined as:

The fraction of a software product's source instruction which changes during a year either through add, delete or modify. ACT is related to the number of change request,

$$ACT = \frac{KLOC_{added} + KLOC_{deleted}}{KLOC_{total}}$$

The **annual maintenance effort (AME)** in person-months is measured as:

$$AME = ACT * SDE$$

Where,

ACT = Annual change traffic,
SDE = Software Development effort in person-months.

Example 7.1: Annual change traffic (ACT) for a software system is 20% per year. The development effort is 700 PMs. Compute an estimate the annual maintenance effort (AME). If the lifetime of the project is 15 years, what is the total effort of the project?

Explanation:

Given,
The development effort = 700PM
Annual Charge traffic (ACT) = 20%
Total duration for which effort is to be calculated = 15 years.

The maintenance effort is a fraction of development effort and that is assumed to be constant

$$AME = ACT * SDE = 0.20 * 700 = 140 \text{ PM}$$

Maintenance effort for 15 years = 15 * 140 = 2100 PM

Thus, the total project effort including maintenance is:

$$\text{Total Effort} = 700+2100=2800 \text{ PM}$$

7.4.5   TAUTE MAINTENANCE MODEL

The **Taute Model** views software maintenance as a **closed-loop process** with eight cyclic phases (e.g., problem identification, analysis, design of change, implementation, testing, documentation update, release, and feedback).

Key idea:

- Maintenance is **continuous**: feedback from each release feeds the next maintenance cycle.

- Emphasizes monitoring, feedback, and incremental improvement.

7.4.6   BELADY AND LEHMAN MODEL

Belady and Lehman studied long-term software evolution and concluded that **poor development and maintenance practices** lead to rapidly increasing effort and cost.

They expressed the growth of maintenance effort with a simplified relation:

$$M = P + Ke^{(c-d)}$$

where:

- M = total maintenance effort

- P = original development effort
- K = constant representing other influencing factors
- c, d = parameters related to quality of development and rate of change

The key takeaway is not the exact formula but the **trend**: if software is poorly designed and not properly controlled, maintenance cost tends to grow **exponentially** with time and change.

7.5 REVERSE ENGINEERING

Reverse engineering involves analyzing an existing software system to understand its structure, functionality, and behavior. This process is often used to improve or modify legacy systems when documentation is insufficient or unavailable. The goal of reverse engineering is to extract knowledge from the software system, which can be used to re-engineer, enhance, or modernize it.

Common Applications:

- **Legacy System Modernization**: Reverse engineering is commonly used to modernize outdated systems without starting from scratch.

- **Understanding Third-Party Code**: It helps in understanding and maintaining software developed by external vendors or third-party developers.

- **Security Audits**: Discovering vulnerabilities, backdoors, or malicious code.

7.5.1 REVERSE ENGINEERING PROCESS:

1. **Information Extraction**:

   Gathering all available information about the system, including source code, binaries, and documentation. If source code is unavailable, DE compilation tools may be used to extract the system's logic from executable files.

2. **Analysis**:

   During the analysis phase, engineers study the system to understand its behaviour, structure, and dependencies. This analysis may involve reviewing algorithms, data structures, design patterns, and relationships between components.

3. **Reconstruction**:

   Based on the analysis, the system's high-level architecture is reconstructed. This includes diagrams, flowcharts, and other documentation that represent the inner workings of the system.

4. **Re-documentation**:

   Proper documentation is created to explain the system's functionality and architecture. This ensures future developers and maintainers can understand and work with the system effectively.

5. **Improvement and Modification**:

   After understanding the system, engineers can make modifications, such as adding new features, optimizing performance, or correcting defects.

Reverse engineering does **not** necessarily change the system itself; it primarily recovers knowledge. Changes occur when reverse engineering is combined with **re-engineering**.

7.6 SOFTWARE RE-ENGINEEIRNG

Software re-engineering refers to the process of examining and modifying an existing system to transform it into a more efficient, maintainable, or modern form. Re-engineering includes processes such as **reverse engineering**, **code restructuring**, and **forward engineering**.

Steps in Re-engineering:

1. **Reverse Engineering**: Analyze the system to understand its architecture and components.

2. **Restructuring**: Modify the internal structure of the software to improve its readability, maintainability, and efficiency.

3. **Re-documentation**: Update or create new documentation to reflect the changes made during re-engineering.

4. **Forward Engineering**: Implement the necessary changes or upgrades to create an improved version of the software. Test and deploy the improved system.

7.6.1   BENEFITS OF SOFTWARE RE-ENGINEERING:

1. **Cost Efficiency**:

Cost-effective than developing a completely new system from scratch.

2. **Improved Software Quality**:

By addressing inefficiencies, performance issues, and maintainability problems, improves the quality and reliability of the software.

3. **Risk Mitigation**:

Re-engineering reduces the risks associated with maintaining outdated or poorly documented systems. By updating both the code and documentation, organizations can ensure that their systems are easier to maintain and modify in the future.

4. **Adaptability**:

Re-engineered systems can be more easily adapted to future business requirements or technological advancements. They are more flexible and can support new features, platforms, or environments without significant overhauls.

7.7 CONFIGURATION MANAGEMENT

Software Configuration Management (SCM) is a set of processes and practices used to control and track changes to software systems. It ensures that changes are systematically managed, and the integrity of the system is maintained throughout its lifecycle.

SCM is essential in complex projects where multiple people work on different parts of the system simultaneously. It also becomes critical when updates and maintenance activities are frequent, as it helps prevent conflicts and inconsistencies in the code.

There are four fundamental sources of change in software:

- **New business or market conditions** dictate changes in product requirements or business rules.
- **New stakeholder needs** demand modification of data produced by systems, functionality delivered by products, or services delivered by the system.
- **Reorganization or business growth/downsizing** causes changes in project priorities or software engineering team structure.
- **Budgetary or scheduling constraints** cause a redefinition of the system or product.

Key Components of SCM:

- **Version Control**: Manages different versions of software to track changes and prevent conflicts.

- **Change Management:** Controls how changes are introduced to the system, ensuring they are tested and approved before implementation.
- **Release Management:** Ensures that new versions or updates are deployed systematically and reliably.
- **Configuration Auditing:** Reviews the configuration of software systems to ensure they meet organizational and project standards.

Tools for Software Configuration Management

There are various SCM tools that automate and facilitate the tasks in SCM, including version control, change tracking, and release management. Some commonly used SCM tools include:

Git: A distributed version control system that allows team members to work on multiple branches and manage merges, with tools like GitHub or GitLab for collaboration.

Subversion (SVN): A centralized version control system that tracks changes in files and directories over time.

Microsoft Team Foundation Server (TFS) / Azure DevOps: An SCM tool that integrates with Visual Studio, providing version control, project tracking, and build automation.

Effective SCM reduces integration problems, supports teamwork, and provides a solid foundation for reliable builds and releases.

7.8 SOFTWARE SUPPLY-CHAIN SECURITY AND PROVENANCE

Recent high-profile cyberattacks targeting build pipelines and open-source package repositories have demonstrated unequivocally that securing only the source code is insufficient in modern software development. Contemporary software systems are assembled from numerous components - third-party libraries, build scripts, container images, and deployment pipelines-forming a complex software supply chain. A critical new research area in software engineering and security focuses on software supply-chain security and provenance, ensuring that every artefact in this chain is both trustworthy and fully traceable throughout its lifecycle.(Hammi et al., 2023)

Frameworks such as in-toto and SLSA (Supply-chain Levels for Software Artefacts) model the build and release process as a sequence of well-defined steps, each producing cryptographically signed metadata documenting what was performed, by whom, and with which inputs. This comprehensive audit trail allows organisations to verify multiple critical security properties throughout the development pipeline.

These verification capabilities include confirming that source code originated from the expected repository and revision, ensuring builds were performed by trusted and isolated builders, validating that binaries and containers correspond exactly to audited source and build steps, and guaranteeing that no unapproved dependencies or malicious modifications infiltrated the pipeline.

Implementing Secure DevOps with Provenance

The integration of supply-chain security extends traditional configuration management into a richer "secure DevOps plus provenance" mindset, which is rapidly becoming a core expectation in large organisations and regulated domains such as finance, healthcare, and government sectors.

These practices represent a fundamental shift in how organisations approach software security. Rather than viewing security as a final gate before deployment, provenance-based approaches embed security verification at every stage of the development pipeline.

01

From Version Control to Provenance Graphs

Configuration management tracks which version is deployed; supply-chain security additionally records how that artefact was produced, providing complete lineage.

02

Assurance Levels for Builds (SLSA)

SLSA defines increasing levels (1–4) of build integrity, progressing from basic provenance recording to fully isolated, reproducible builds with strong cryptographic guarantees.

03

Support for Incident Response

When vulnerabilities are discovered, provenance data enables teams to quickly identify which builds, environments, and customers are affected, accelerating remediation.

04

Link to Maintenance and Evolution

As systems evolve and dependencies change, supply-chain metadata becomes essential for safe upgrading, patching, and maintaining audit readiness throughout the software lifecycle.

This continuous verification model aligns perfectly with modern DevOps practices whilst addressing the sophisticated threats facing contemporary software systems. For software engineering professionals, understanding and implementing these supply-chain security principles has become an essential competency, as critical as version control or testing methodologies.

7.9 SOFTWARE DOCUMENTATION

Software documentation is a written record that describes the design, architecture, functionality, and usage of a software system. Proper documentation is essential for maintaining the system, ensuring that future developers or maintainers can understand and modify the software effectively.

Types of Documentation:

1. **User Documentation**: Guides end users on how to use the software product.

    It Includes, User Manuals, Installation Guides, FAQs, Troubleshooting Guides etc.

2. **System Documentation**: Provides technical details about the system's architecture, code, and design, intended for developers and maintainers.

It Includes, Requirement Specification, Design Documents, Source Code Documentation, API Documentations, Test Documentations etc

Documentation Tools

Several tools are widely used to streamline and manage documentation:

- **Markdown Editors:** Such as MarkdownPad and Typora, for simple, readable documentation.
- **Code Documentation Generators:**
  - *Javadoc* for Java
  - *Doxygen* for multiple languages (C, C++, Java, etc.)
  - *Sphinx* for Python

  These tools generate API documentation directly from annotated source code.

- **Version Control Platforms:** GitHub, GitLab, and Bitbucket for maintaining versions of documentation along with code.
- **Diagramming Tools:** Lucidchart, Draw.io, and Microsoft Visio for creating architectural diagrams and data flowcharts.

Effective documentation reduces the risk of miscommunication, ensures consistency in software development, and facilitates easier maintenance and future enhancements.

7.10 EXERCISES

7.1   What are the various categories of software maintenance?

7.2   Write a short note on the maintenance process with a suitable diagram. What type of software testing is generally used in Software Maintenance?

7.3   Explain the Boehm's maintenance model with the help of a diagram.

7.4   Write short note on the following:
   i.   Re-engineering
   ii.   Reverse Engineering

7.5   Annual Change Traffic for a software is 14% per year. The development effort is 500 PMs. Compute an estimate for Annual Maintenance Effort and total effort, If the life time of the project is 12 years.

7.6   Compare and contrast reverse engineering and software re-engineering. In what situations would you recommend using each approach?

8 AGILE DEVELOPMENT

In many business situations, a **fast turnaround** in software development is essential. Organisations often need a working product soon after specifying requirements in order to respond to market pressures and competitive demands. This is where **Agile Development** becomes important—a family of methods designed to accommodate rapid change and deliver software quickly and iteratively.

Agile represents a shift from traditional, rigid, plan-driven methodologies. It is sometimes informally called *"software engineering lite"* because of its emphasis on:

- Flexibility and responsiveness

- Close customer collaboration

- Iterative, incremental delivery

Unlike linear models such as the Waterfall model, Agile methods are explicitly designed to **welcome change**, even late in the project. At the same time, Agile is **not** a one-size-fits-all solution. Software engineers must still exercise judgment and adapt the process to the specific domain, team size, risk profile and customer needs.

8.1 AGILITY PRINCIPLES

The Agile Alliance, through the **Agile Manifesto**, outlines a set of principles that guide teams in practicing agility. The following twelve principles capture the spirit of Agile development:

1. **Customer satisfaction through early and continuous delivery**
   Deliver valuable working software early and regularly to satisfy the customer.

2. **Welcome changing requirements**
   Even late in development, changes are welcome. Agile processes harness change for the customer's competitive advantage.

3. **Frequent delivery of working software**
   Deliver operational software frequently (from a couple of weeks to a couple of months), with a preference for the shorter timescale.

4. **Close collaboration**
   Business stakeholders and developers must work together daily throughout the project.

5. **Build projects around motivated individuals**
   Give them the environment and support they need and trust them to get the job done.

6. **Face-to-face communication**
   The most efficient and effective method of conveying information within a development team is face-to-face conversation (or its closest practical equivalent).

7. **Working software as the primary measure of progress**
   Documentation and plans are useful, but working software is the key indicator.

8. **Sustainable development**
   Agile processes promote sustainable development. Sponsors, developers and users should be able to maintain a constant pace indefinitely.

9. **Continuous attention to technical excellence and good design**

Good engineering practices and quality design enhance agility.

10. **Simplicity**

Simplicity—the art of maximizing the amount of work **not** done—is essential.

11. **Self-organising teams**

The best architectures, requirements and designs emerge from self-organising teams.

12. **Reflection and adaptation**

At regular intervals, the team reflects on how to become more effective and then tunes and adjusts its behaviour accordingly.

These principles form the conceptual foundation of Agile software engineering. Their practical implementation may vary depending on project constraints, domain and organisational culture.

For further reading on the underlying philosophy, see the **Agile Manifesto** (Beck et al., 2001)

8.2 RAPID SOFTWARE DEVELOPMENT (RAD)

Rapid Application Development (RAD) is a methodology focused on delivering software quickly through iterative and incremental development. RAD uses techniques such as prototyping, component-based development, and visual programming tools to accelerate the development process.

An analogy to understand RAD is the construction of a **bridge or dam**: Unlike software development, where changes and improvements can be made incrementally, such structures must be fully functional from the outset. In software, rapid delivery is often necessary to remain competitive, even if it means sacrificing some aspects of quality temporarily. Non-functional requirements (e.g., performance, security) can be improved over time as the product matures.

The goal of RAD is to have working software available quickly, showing progress to stakeholders while the remaining functionality is delivered in stages. For a more in-depth understanding, the book **"Rapid Development: Taming Wild Software Schedules"** (McConnell, 2010) is a great resource.

8.3 AGILE METHODS

There are several popular agile methodologies, each with its own approach to software development:

- ➢ Extreme Programming (XP)
- ➢ SCRUM
- ➢ Crystal
- ➢ Adaptive Software Development (ASD)

Each method has its own emphasis and practices but shares the common Agile values of incremental delivery, customer collaboration and responsiveness to change.

8.3.1 EXTREME PROGRAMMING (XP)

Extreme Programming (XP), introduced by **Kent Beck**, (Beck, 1999) emphasizes collaboration between customers and developers to keep the process simple and responsive. XP encourages developers to focus on current needs without worrying too much about future changes, as requirements may evolve.

XP identifies four key control variables:

- **Cost, Time, Quality and Scope**

XP's success is built around five core values:

1. **Communication**

2. **Simplicity**
3. **Feedback**
4. **Courage**
5. **Respect**

XP is an **iterative** process. The project is divided into a sequence of mini-projects or **releases**, each resulting in a working version of the software. Feedback is collected continually, and **frequent releases** (every one to three months) ensure that the product remains aligned with business needs.

Key XP practices include:

- Small, frequent releases
- Test-driven development (TDD)
- Pair programming
- Continuous integration
- Simple design and constant refactoring

Release planning is typically done through **Planning Games**, where:

- The **customer** defines and prioritises the features (user stories) to be included in a release.

- The **developers** estimate the effort required and indicate how much can be realistically delivered within the available time.

In some cases, the customer fixes the **scope** and the developers estimate the **time**; in others, the customer fixes the **time-box** and the developers commit to a realistic subset of features.

Each release is broken into short **iterations** (usually not more than three weeks), each of which results in a stable, integrated build.

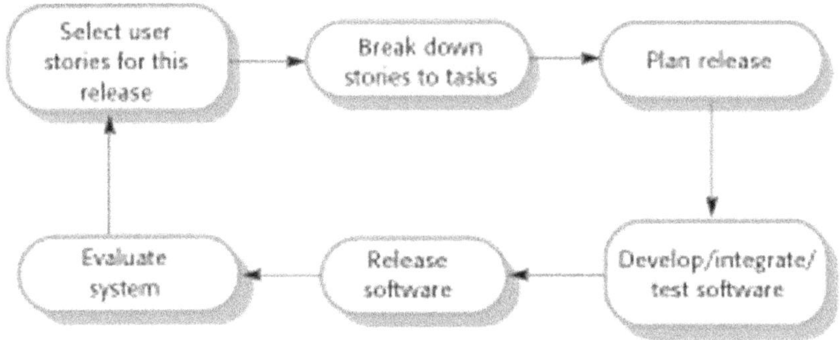

Figure 62: XP Development Process Cycle

8.3.2   SCRUM

Scrum, developed by Jeff Sutherland and others in the early 1990s, is an Agile framework centred around **sprints**—short, time-boxed iterations (typically 2–4 weeks) during which the team delivers a potentially shippable product increment.

Key Scrum roles:
- **Product Owner** – Manages the Product Backlog and prioritises features according to business value.
- **Scrum Master** – Facilitates the process, removes impediments and ensures Scrum practices are followed.
- **Development Team** – A self-organising, cross-functional team that plans and executes the work within each sprint.

Within each sprint, the team performs:

- Sprint Planning
- Design and development
- Testing and integration
- Sprint Review (demonstration to stakeholders)
- Sprint Retrospective (reflection and process improvement)

Scrum is particularly suitable for projects where requirements can **change rapidly**, as the backlog can be reprioritised at the start of each sprint.

Further reading: **"Scrum: The Art of Doing Twice the Work in Half the Time"** (Sutherland, 2014).

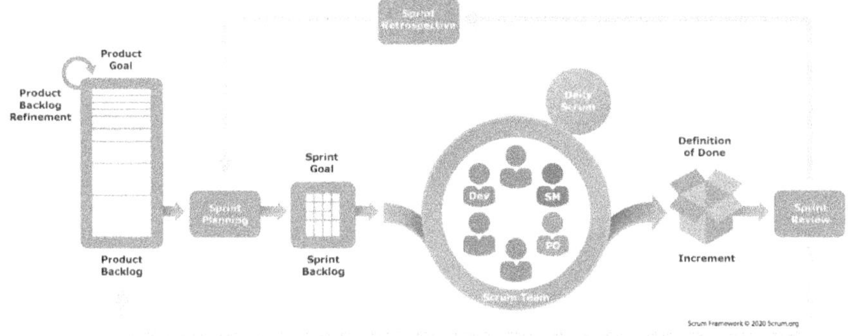

Figure 63: Scrum Framework

8.3.3 CRYSTAL

Crystal is a **family** of Agile methodologies tailored to different team sizes and criticality levels (e.g., Crystal Clear, Crystal Orange). Crystal places strong emphasis on:

- Frequent delivery
- Reflective improvement
- Osmotic communication (easy, informal information flow)
- Simplicity and light documentation

Crystal recognises that different projects need different levels of rigor, and it adapts practices accordingly. Its lightweight nature makes it especially suitable for small to medium-sized teams.

8.3.4 Adaptive Software Development (ASD)

Adaptive Software Development (ASD) focuses on rapid delivery and adaptability. Like other agile methods, ASD values working software over documentation and emphasizes collaboration between developers, customers, and stakeholders. Frequent iterations and continuous feedback ensure the product remains aligned with evolving business needs.

For further study, consider **"Adaptive Software Development: A Collaborative Approach to Managing Complex Systems"** (Highsmith, 2000).

8.4 TESTING IN AGILE DEVELOPMENT

Testing is an integral part of Agile development. In contrast to traditional models, where testing is done after development, Agile testing occurs **concurrently** with development. The **testing team** works on test scenarios and scripts as developers code the modules. This parallel approach ensures that feedback loops are short, allowing for rapid identification and correction of issues.

Types of Testing in Agile:

- **Unit Testing**: Verifies that individual components function as expected.

- **Integration Testing**: Ensures that different components work well together.

- **System Testing**: Tests the entire system to validate end-to-end scenarios.

- **Smoke Testing**: A preliminary test to check basic functionality.

- **Regression Testing**: Ensures that new changes do not break existing functionality.

- **Performance Testing**: Evaluates system performance under load.

- **Exploratory Testing**: Involves testers exploring the system without predefined test cases.

- **Acceptance Testing**: Verifies that the software meets business requirements and is ready for release.

For more in-depth knowledge on Agile testing, refer to **"Agile Testing: A Practical Guide for Testers and Agile Teams"** (Crispin et al., 2009)

8.4.1 CASELET: AGILE IN A COLLEGE PROJECT TEAM

A group of four B.Tech students decide to build an **Online Assignment Submission Portal** as their final-year project. Initially, they try to write a detailed 30–40 page SRS and full design before starting any code, but their guide warns them that the requirements may keep changing (new features requested by faculty, changes in evaluation pattern, etc.).

On the guide's suggestion, they shift to a **lightweight Agile approach**:

- They split the project into **small user stories**, such as:

  - "As a teacher, I want to create an assignment with a deadline."

  - "As a student, I want to upload my solution and see submission status."

- They plan **2-week iterations**. At the end of each iteration, they must show **working software**, even if only a small part of the total system.

- The CR of the class and two faculty members play the role of **stakeholders**, giving feedback every two weeks.

In the **first iteration**, the team delivers a very basic portal: teacher login, create assignment, and a simple student upload feature. Immediately, faculty ask for:

- Late-submission marking
- Automatic PDF merging of all submissions
- A basic plagiarism warning

Instead of rewriting a large design document, the team simply updates the **product backlog** and plans the next iteration. Every cycle they:

1. Pick the highest priority items from the backlog
2. Implement and **unit test** them
3. Do a short **system demo** to the guide and faculty
4. Note bugs and improvement suggestions for the next iteration

By the end of the semester, even though requirements changed multiple times, the team has a **working, deployed portal** on the college intranet.

This case illustrates how Agile practices—**small iterations, close stakeholder feedback, and working software as the main measure of progress**—helped the team handle changing requirements without losing control of the project.

8.5 EXERCISES

8.1. What is agile software development? Outline the agile process and discuss its relevance in the present software development.

8.2. Discuss Agility Principles

8.3. List the different types of testing techniques used in agile software engineering and write the significance of each testing technique.

8.4. Explain the key differences between traditional software development methodologies and Agile Development. Why is Agile considered more suitable for projects with rapidly changing requirements?

8.5. Compare and contrast the Extreme Programming (XP) and Scrum methodologies. Highlight their core differences in terms of project management, iteration cycles and team collaboration.

9   COMPUTER AIDED SOFTWARE ENGINEERING (CASE)

Computer-Aided Software Engineering (CASE) refers to the use of computer-based tools and environments to assist in software development and maintenance. These tools are designed to make software engineering tasks easier, more efficient, and more reliable.

By automating certain processes, CASE tools reduce the time, effort, and potential errors involved in software development, contributing to improved productivity and software quality.

9.1   CASE TOOLS

A CASE tool is a software product designed to support one or more stages of the software development lifecycle (SDLC). These tools are used to automate tasks such as requirement gathering, system design, code generation, testing, and documentation, among others.

9.1.1   CASE TOOLS BENEFITS

- **Increase Productivity:** Automates repetitive tasks, allowing developers to focus on complex and creative work.
- **Improve software quality:** Ensures consistency, reduces human errors, and adheres to best practices throughout the development process.
- **Help communication between Team:** Enhances collaboration among development team members by offering shared documentation, repositories, and standards.

- **Reduction of time and effort**
  - Tasks such as diagram creation, testing, and documentation are automated, making them faster to complete and modify.
  - Reduces both development and long-term maintenance costs by providing consistency and automation.

9.1.2 CONCERNS IN ADOPTING CASE TOOLS

- **Maintenance Challenges:** CASE tools themselves may require maintenance and updates, adding to the workload.
- **High Costs:** The cost of acquiring, implementing, and training staff on CASE tools can be significant.
- **Training Requirements:** Using CASE tools often requires specialized training, which may take time and add expenses to a project.
- **Template Incompatibility:** Documentation templates provided by CASE tools may not align with an organization's specific needs or existing standards.
- **Integration Difficulties:** Combining different tools to support the full software development lifecycle can be difficult, and moving data between tools may not be seamless.
- **Lack of Standardization:** Transferring data between different CASE tools is often difficult, as there is no common interchange format.

9.1.3 CATEGORIES OF CASE TOOLS

- **Front-End Tools:** These support the initial phases of the software development lifecycle, such as requirements gathering, system analysis, and design.
  - Example: Diagramming tools for flowcharts, data models, and system architecture.

- **Back-End Tools:** These assist in later stages like implementation, testing, and maintenance.

  Example: Tools for database generation, test automation, and compilers.

- **Integrated CASE (I-CASE):** These tools provide support for the entire software development lifecycle, integrating both front-end and back-end functions into a cohesive environment.

  Example: Complete development suites that combine modeling, code generation, version control, and testing tools with a common repository.

9.1.4 TYPES OF CASE TOOLS

Intelligent Diagramming Tools: Used to represent data and system processes during system analysis and design. It represents control flow and data flow among different software components and system structures. **For example,** Tools for creating flowcharts and data flow diagrams (DFDs).

Report Generators: These help in understanding the data requirements and the relationships involved. **Example:** Crystal Report

Central Repository: It provides a single point of storage for data diagrams, reports, and documents related to project management. **Example:** Unified Modeling Language (UML) repositories.

Documentation Generators: It helps in generating user and technical documentation as per standards. It creates documents for technical users and end users. **Example:** DrExplain, Adobe RoboHelp for documentation.

Code Generators: It aids in the auto-generation of code, including definitions, with the help of designs, documents, and diagrams. **Example:** Model-driven development (MDD) tools that convert UML diagrams into executable code.

Prototyping: Prototyping CASE tools helps in populating data dictionary and ensure consistency between design and prototype. Prototyping CASE tool also supports to create a GUI using a graphics editor and define data forms, menus and controls. Run time system of prototype should support mock runs of input and output data. **Example:** Tools for designing graphical user interfaces (GUIs), such as Axure and Balsamiq.

9.1.5 AI-AUGMENTED SOFTWARE DEVELOPMENT WITH LARGE LANGUAGE MODELS

Over the last few years, large language models (LLMs) for code have emerged as a transformative force in software engineering, representing a new class of powerful Computer-Aided Software Engineering (CASE) tools. These sophisticated models, such as Code Llama, Codex, and similar systems, are trained on massive corpora of source code and natural language documentation, enabling them to assist developers across almost every phase of the software development life cycle. This breakthrough has fundamentally changed how we approach software construction and maintenance. (Jiang et al., 2018)

Instead of writing all code manually from scratch, developers can now describe the required functionality in natural language and request the LLM to suggest code implementations, test cases, documentation comments, or refactorings. This paradigm shift has given rise to the concept of AI-augmented software development, where the human developer maintains control of critical design decisions and review processes, whilst the LLM automates numerous low-level or repetitive tasks. This collaboration between human expertise and machine intelligence represents a significant evolution in software engineering practice, promising substantial improvements in both productivity and code quality.

9.1.5.1 *Key Roles of LLM-Based Tools in Software Engineering*

Large language models have proven remarkably versatile across the entire software development lifecycle, offering assistance that spans from initial requirements gathering through to final deployment and maintenance. Early empirical studies demonstrate significant improvements in developer productivity and satisfaction, though they also highlight important risks such as incorrect or insecure code suggestions, licence concerns, and the potential for over-reliance on automated tools.

Requirements and Design Support

Generate draft user stories, use-case descriptions, design alternatives, and quick prototypes from informal problem statements. This accelerates the initial planning phases significantly.

Coding Assistance

Provide intelligent code completion, full function suggestions, API usage examples, and language migration support (e.g., from Java to Python), reducing repetitive coding tasks.

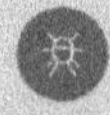

Testing and Debugging

Propose comprehensive unit tests and boundary test cases, explain failing tests with contextual insights, and suggest possible fixes based on error messages or stack traces.

Documentation and Review

Generate API documentation automatically, summarise code changes in pull requests, and highlight potential code smells or security vulnerabilities before they reach production.

For students and aspiring software engineers, LLM-based assistants should be viewed as the next generation of CASE tools, sitting alongside traditional diagram editors, code generators, and test frameworks. However, it is crucial to emphasise that these tools always require critical human judgement and oversight. The developer's role evolves from pure code authorship to that of an informed reviewer and architect, making strategic decisions whilst leveraging AI for tactical implementation support. This collaborative model represents the future of software development, where human creativity and machine efficiency work in harmony.

9.1.6   CASE ENVIRONMENT

A **CASE Environment** refers to an integrated collection of CASE tools designed to support the entire software development lifecycle. The main advantage of a CASE environment is that it allows for seamless interaction between tools and the automation of multiple development steps.

A complete CASE environment typically includes:

- Tools for requirements gathering, design, code generation, testing, and maintenance.
- A central repository for storing all project-related artifacts.
- Mechanisms for integrating the activities and data flow between different phases of software development.

Difference from a Programming Environment:

- A **Programming Environment** is focused only on coding and compilation, while
- A **CASE Environment** supports the entire lifecycle, from initial planning through to deployment and maintenance.

9.2 NO CODE TOOLS

No-Code platforms are a class of development tools that allow users to build software applications without writing any code, using drag-and-drop interfaces to configure functionality. While no-code tools streamline application development, they are not a substitute for software development methodologies such as Agile. Instead, no-code platforms are **tools** that can be integrated into agile projects to accelerate development without needing programming skills.

9.2.1   BENEFITS OF NO-CODE TOOLS

- **Faster Development**: Developers and even non-technical users can build applications quickly.

- **Lower Development Costs**: No-code platforms reduce the need for hiring expensive developers, which is particularly beneficial for small businesses.
- **Improved Collaboration**: Non-technical team members can actively participate in the development process.

9.2.2 POPULAR NO-CODE TOOLS

- **Webflow**: A website builder that allows designers to create responsive websites visually.

- **Bubble**: A comprehensive platform for building web applications with no coding required.

- **Wix**: A popular drag-and-drop website builder.

- **Zapier**: A tool for automating workflows by connecting various apps and services.

- **Airtable**: A tool for building databases with a simple, spreadsheet-like interface.

- **Glide**: A platform for building mobile applications using Google Sheets.

- **Unbounce**: A platform for creating high-converting landing pages without needing technical expertise.

Each tool targets different use cases—such as web design, process automation, data management, and app prototyping—and can be used to build Minimum Viable Products (MVPs) or proof-of-concept systems before committing to full-scale development.

9.3 CONCLUSION

Computer-Aided Software Engineering (CASE) tools and environments, along with emerging no-code platforms, have significantly transformed the way software is developed and maintained. CASE tools primarily focus on automating and supporting key phases of the software development life cycle, ensuring consistency, improving quality, and reducing effort.

No-code platforms, on the other hand, empower non-developers to contribute directly to application creation through visual interfaces and configuration rather than traditional coding. When used appropriately, both CASE tools and no-code platforms:

- Enhance team collaboration
- Improve software quality and consistency
- Reduce development and maintenance time
- Shorten time-to-market

Together, they form an important part of the modern software engineering toolkit.

9.4 EXERCISES

1. Define CASE tools. What is their primary purpose in software engineering?
2. Discuss three major challenges organizations may face when adopting CASE tools. How can these challenges be mitigated?
3. Differentiate between front-end tools, back-end tools, and integrated CASE (I-CASE) tools. Provide examples for each.
4. Explain the role of code generators in CASE. How do they help reduce development time and improve software quality?
5. What are no-code tools, and how do they differ from traditional programming tools? List at least three no-code tools and describe their primary use cases.

10   Annexure A

10.1 IMPORTANT DEFINITIONS AND KEY TERMS

1. **Software Development Life Cycle (SDLC)**

   A structured sequence of phases (such as requirements, design, implementation, testing, deployment, and maintenance) used to develop and maintain software systematically.

2. **Software Requirements Specification (SRS)**

   A formal document that describes **what** the software system will do, including functional and non-functional requirements, interfaces, constraints, and assumptions, without specifying how it will be implemented.

3. **Functional Requirement**

   A requirement that describes **behaviour** of the system—what the system should do in terms of inputs, processing, and outputs (e.g., "System shall generate monthly fee reports").

4. **Non-Functional Requirement**

   A requirement that specifies **how** the system should perform rather than what it does, such as performance, reliability, usability, security, maintainability, and portability.

5. **Use Case**

A description of a sequence of interactions between an **actor** (user or external system) and the software system to achieve a specific goal, written at the level of system behaviour ("what", not "how").

6. **Data Flow Diagram (DFD)**

A graphical model that shows **how data moves** through a system: from external entities, through processes, into and out of data stores, using standard symbols for processes, data flows, data stores, and external entities.

7. **Entity–Relationship (ER) Diagram**

A conceptual data model that represents **entities** (things about which data is stored), their **attributes**, and the **relationships** between them, used to design and understand the logical structure of a database.

8. **Modularity**
The property of a software system being decomposed into **independent, well-defined modules** with clear interfaces, making the system easier to understand, implement, test, and maintain.

9. **Coupling**
A measure of the **degree of interdependence** between software modules. High coupling means modules share a lot of data or control; low coupling (desired) means modules interact through minimal, well-defined interfaces.

10. **Cohesion**
A measure of how strongly the elements within a module are **related to one another**. High cohesion (desired) means a module performs one well-defined task or a set of closely related tasks; low cohesion indicates a mixed, unrelated collection of responsibilities.

11. **Software Design**

   The process of transforming requirements into a **blueprint for construction**, covering architecture (high-level structure), module design, data structures, interfaces, and algorithms that can be implemented in code.

12. **Verification**
   The process of checking whether work products of a development phase **meet the specifications** imposed at the start of that phase. It answers: *"Are we building the product right?"* (e.g., reviews, inspections, static analysis).

13. **Validation**
   The process of evaluating the final software to ensure it **meets user needs and requirements**. It answers: *"Are we building the right product?"* (e.g., system testing, acceptance testing).

14. **Black-Box (Functional) Testing**

   A testing approach that focuses on **inputs and outputs** of the software without knowledge of its internal code or structure, to check whether the system behaviour matches the specified functional requirements.

15. **White-Box (Structural) Testing**

   A testing approach that examines the **internal structure, logic, and code** of the software. Test cases are designed to exercise statements, branches, conditions, loops, and internal data structures.

16. **Integration Testing**

   A level of testing in which **individually tested modules are combined and tested as a group** to detect interface errors, data flow issues, and control flow problems that arise when components interact.

17. **Acceptance Testing (Alpha and Beta)**

The final testing phase to determine whether the software is **ready for operational use** and satisfies business requirements.

- o**Alpha Testing:** Performed at the developer's site, in a controlled environment, usually by internal users.

- o**Beta Testing:** Performed by real users at their own sites, in a live environment, to uncover issues not found earlier.

18. **Debugging**
The process of **identifying, isolating, and correcting** the cause of a failure or defect after testing reveals symptoms of an error, followed by re-testing to ensure the fix works and does not introduce new problems.

19. **Software Reliability**

The **probability that software will operate without failure** for a specified period under specified conditions. It reflects the ability of a system or component to perform its required functions consistently and correctly.

20. **Fault, Error, Bug and Failure**

- o**Fault:** A static defect in the code or design (wrong or missing logic).

- o**Error:** An incorrect internal state when a fault is executed.

- o**Bug:** Informal term for a defect that causes incorrect or unexpected behaviour.

- o**Failure:** Observable deviation of the system from its required behaviour when an error propagates to the output.

21. **COCOMO (Constructive Cost Model)**
A family of empirical models proposed by Barry Boehm for **estimating software development effort and schedule** based on project size (KLOC/DSI) and cost drivers. Includes Basic, Intermediate, and Detailed/COCOMO II variants, and modes such as organic, semi-detached, and embedded.

22. **Putnam Resource Allocation / Rayleigh Curve**
A software project staffing model based on the **Rayleigh–Norden manpower distribution**, describing how effort gradually increases, peaks, and then decreases over the project life, and relating total effort, schedule, and staffing.

23. **Software Maintenance and Its Categories**
All activities undertaken after delivery to **correct faults, improve performance, or adapt** the software to a changed environment. Maintenance is typically classified as: **Corrective**, **Adaptive**, **Perfective**, and **Preventive** maintenance.

24. **Agile Software Development:** A family of iterative and incremental methods that emphasize **customer collaboration, responsiveness to change, working software, and small, self-organising teams**. Examples include Extreme Programming (XP), Scrum, Crystal, and Adaptive Software Development.

25. **CASE Tools (Computer-Aided Software Engineering Tools)**
Software products that **support one or more phases** of the software development lifecycle (requirements, design, coding, testing, documentation, maintenance) by automating tasks, enforcing consistency, and improving productivity.

10.2 IMPORTANT FORMULAE AND MODELS

---

1. Basic COCOMO Effort and Schedule Equations

For a project of size **KLOC** (thousands of delivered source instructions):

- **Effort (person-months)**

$$E = a \times (\text{KLOC})^b$$

- **Development Time / Schedule (months)**

$$S = c \times (E)^d$$

Typical constants for **Basic COCOMO** (Mode-wise):

Mode	Effort E	Schedule S
Organic	$E = 2.4 \times (\text{KLOC})^{1.05}$	$S = 2.5 \times E^{0.38}$
Semi-detached	$E = 3.0 \times (\text{KLOC})^{1.12}$	$S = 2.5 \times E^{0.35}$
Embedded	$E = 3.6 \times (\text{KLOC})^{1.20}$	$S = 2.5 \times E^{0.32}$

Productivity and average staffing (if size is in DSI):

$$\text{Productivity} = \frac{\text{DSI}}{E} \qquad \text{Average Staffing} = \frac{E}{S}$$

---

2. Intermediate COCOMO with Effort Adjustment Factor (EAF)

- **Effort (person-months)**

$$E = a \times (\text{KLOC})^b \times \text{EAF}$$

- **Development Time (months)**

$$S = c \times (E)^d$$

Where **EAF (Effort Adjustment Factor)** is the product of 15 cost driver multipliers:

$$EAF = \prod_{i=1}^{15} CD_i$$

Mode-wise constants (Intermediate Model):

Mode	a	b	c	d
Organic	3.2	1.05	2.5	0.38
Semi-detached	3.0	1.12	2.5	0.35
Embedded	2.8	1.20	2.5	0.32

3. Reliability – Series System Allocation

For **n components in series** (all must work for system to work), overall reliability is:

$$R_S = \prod_{i=1}^{n} R_i$$

For three components:

$$R_S = R_1 \times R_2 \times R_3$$

If a total **cost function** is used in allocation:

$$C_T = C_1(R_1) + C_2(R_2) + C_3(R_3)$$

Optimum allocation chooses R_1, R_2, R_3 to satisfy the reliability target (e.g., $R_S \geq 0.95$) with minimum C_T.

4. Putnam / Rayleigh Manpower Model

Let:

- $m(t)$: manpower usage rate at time t

- $y(t)$: cumulative manpower up to time t

- K: total effort (area under the curve)

- a, k: model parameters

Rayleigh manpower curve:

$$m(t) = \frac{dy}{dt} = 2kate^{-at^2}$$

On integration:

$$y(t) = K(1 - e^{-at^2})$$

with boundary conditions $y(0) = 0$, $y(\infty) = K$.

---

5. Musa's Basic Execution Time Model

Parameters:

- $\lambda(\mu)$: current failure intensity (failures per unit execution time)
- λ_0: initial failure intensity
- μ: mean number of failures experienced so far
- V_0: total expected failures in infinite time
- τ: execution time

Failure intensity as a function of mean failures:

$$\lambda(\mu) = \lambda_0\left(1 - \frac{\mu}{V_0}\right)$$

Rate of change of failure intensity:

$$\frac{d\lambda}{d\mu} = -\frac{\lambda_0}{V_0}$$

Mean failures as a function of execution time:

$$\mu(\tau) = V_0(1 - e^{-\frac{\lambda_0 \tau}{V_0}})$$

Failure intensity as a function of execution time:

$$\lambda(\tau) = \lambda_0\, e^{-\frac{\lambda_0 \tau}{V_0}}$$

Additional failures and time to move from λ_1 to target λ_2:

$$\Delta\mu = \frac{V_0}{\lambda_0}(\lambda_1 - \lambda_2)$$

$$\Delta\tau = \frac{V_0}{\lambda_0}\ln\left(\frac{\lambda_1}{\lambda_2}\right)$$

---

6. Musa–Okumoto Logarithmic Poisson Model

Parameters:

- $\lambda(\mu)$: failure intensity
- λ_0: initial failure intensity
- θ: decay parameter

Failure intensity vs. cumulative failures:

$$\lambda(\mu) = \lambda_0 e^{-\theta\mu}$$

Rate of change of failure intensity:

$$\frac{d\lambda}{d\mu} = -\theta\lambda_0 e^{-\theta\mu} = -\theta\lambda(\mu)$$

---

7. Cyclomatic Complexity (McCabe)

Given a control flow graph G with:

- E: number of edges
- N: number of nodes
- P: number of connected components

Cyclomatic Complexity:

$$V(G) = E - N + 2P$$

Properties:
- $V(G) \geq 1$
- $V(G)$ = number of linearly independent paths
- $V(G)$ = number of regions in the flow graph (including the outer region)

The minimum number of test cases for full path coverage is **at least** $V(G)$.

---

8. Boehm's Maintenance Effort Formula (ACT)

Let:
- **ACT**: Annual Change Traffic (fraction of source instructions changed per year)

- **SDE**: Software Development Effort (person-months)

- **AME**: Annual Maintenance Effort (person-months)

Then:

$$AME = ACT \times SDE$$

Total maintenance effort over T years:

$$\text{Total Maintenance Effort} = T \times AME$$

Total project effort including development:

$$\text{Total Effort} = SDE + T \times AME$$

REFERENCES

Aggarwal, K. K. (2005). *Software engineering*. New Age International.

Beck, K. (1999). Embracing change with extreme programming. *Computer*, *32*(10), 70–77.

Beck, K., Beedle, M., Bennekum, A. Van, Cockburn, A., Cunningham, W., Fowler, M., Grenning, J., Highsmith, J., Hunt, A., Jeffries, R., Kern, J., Marick, B., Martin, R. C., Mellor, S., Schwaber, K., Sutherland, J., & Thomas, D. (2001). *Manifesto for Agile Software Development*. The Agile Alliance.

Bhatia, P. K., Mittal, H. K., & Singla, K. (2010). HANDLING IMPRECISION IN SOFTWARE ENGINEERING MEASUREMNTS USING FUZZY LOGIC. *Dronacharya Research Journal* , *II*, 51–57.

Boehm, B. W. (1988). A spiral model of software development and enhancement. *Computer*, *21*(5), 61–72.

Boehm, B. W. (1991). Software risk management: principles and practices. *IEEE Software*, *8*(1), 32–41.

Botten, N. A. (1994). Development process assessment toward leading edge quality. *IEEE Journal on Selected Areas in Communications*, *12*(2), 251–257.

Brooks Jr, F. P. (1995). *The mythical man-month: essays on software engineering*. Pearson Education.

Crispin, L., Gregory, J., Lead, A. P., Mentor, O., & Services, I. K. (2009). Agile Testing: A Practical Guide for Testers and Agile Teams. In *Vasa*.

Hammi, B., Zeadally, S., & Nebhen, J. (2023). Security Threats, Countermeasures, and Challenges of Digital Supply Chains. *ACM Computing Surveys*, *55*(14 S). https://doi.org/10.1145/3588999;SUBPAGE:STRING:ABSTRACT; WEBSITE:WEBSITE:DL-SITE;REQUESTEDJOURNAL:JOURNAL:CSUR;TAXONOMY:TAX ONOMY:ACM-PUBTYPE;PAGEGROUP:STRING:PUBLICATION

Henry, S., & Kafura, D. (1981). Software structure metrics based on information flow. *IEEE Transactions on Software Engineering*, *5*, 510–518.

Highsmith, J. A. (2000). Adaptive Software Development: A Collaborative Approach to Managing Complex Systems. In *Journal of Evolutionary Biology* (Vol. 12).

Jia, Y., & Harman, M. (2011). An analysis and survey of the development of mutation testing. *IEEE Transactions on Software Engineering*, *37*(5), 649–678. https://doi.org/10.1109/TSE.2010.62

Jiang, J., Wang, F., Shen, J., Kim, S., & Kim, S. (2018). A Survey on Large Language Models for Code Generation. *J. ACM*, *37*(4). https://arxiv.org/pdf/2406.00515

Mall, R. (2018). *Fundamentals of software engineering*. PHI Learning Pvt. Ltd.

McConnell, S. (2010). Rapid Development: Taming Wild Software Schedules. *Microsoft Press*, 6.

Musa, J. D., & Okumoto, K. (1983). Software Reliability Models: Concepts, Classification, Comparisons, and Practice. *NATO ASI Series, Series F: Computer and Systems Sciences*, *3*, 395–423. https://doi.org/10.1007/978-3-642-82014-4_22

Paulk, M. C., Curtis, B., & Chrissis, M. B. (1991). *Capability maturity model for software*.

Pressman, R. S. (2005). *Software engineering: a practitioner's approach*. Palgrave macmillan.

Putnam, L. H. (1978). A general empirical solution to the macro software sizing and estimating problem. *IEEE Transactions on Software Engineering*, *4*, 345–361.

Sommerville, I. (2005). Integrated requirements engineering: A tutorial. *IEEE Software*, *22*(1), 16–23.

Sutherland, J. (2014). Scrum : The Art of Doing Twice the Work in Half the Time. In *Crown*.